# Discovery Walks in Cornwall

## Alexandra J. Pratt

**Published by** Sigma Leisure – an imprint of Sigma Press, 1 South Oak Lane, Wilmslow, Cheshire SK9 6AR, England.

**British Library Cataloguing in Publication Data**
A CIP record for this book is available from the British Library.

**ISBN:** 1-85058-632-2


**Typesetting and Design by:** Sigma Press, Wilmslow, Cheshire.


**Cover:** Merry Maidens Stone Circle, Penwith; Porthleven Beach; the author on Marazion Beach, with St Michael's Mount in the background.

**Maps:** Jeremy Semmens

**Photographs:** the author

**Printed by:** MFP Design and Print

**Reprinted** 2000

**Disclaimer:** the information in this book is given in good faith and is believed to be correct at the time of publication. No responsibility is accepted by either the author or publisher for errors or omissions, or for any loss or injury howsoever caused. Only you can judge your own fitness, competence and experience.

# Preface

This book introduces those new to Cornwall and old hands to the county's secret places; landscapes untouched by roads and ancient monuments not defaced by modern hands. The diversity of landscape in this, England's most remote county, is truly astonishing and offers some of the best walking in England for all levels of fitness. Visitors come to this rich and fertile corner for many reasons: the warm climate, which supports some of the country's best subtropical gardens, nature's riot of colour, especially in the spring and summer and the tranquillity far from the stress and pollution of modern life.

As a rule, no walk should be attempted without a suitable map, and the relevant ones are listed at the start of each route. In particular, for several of the walks in Penwith and on Bodmin Moor a map is indispensable and a compass is highly recommended. All routes have been walked and checked by the author and this guide-book has been written using public rights of way and permissive paths (clearly marked). However, neither the author nor the publisher can accept responsibility for any changes to the status of routes, or any errors that may have inadvertently crept into the route descriptions.

The walking grades given at the start of each walk are based on the ability of a fairly active adult, and even those graded as challenging should present no difficulty for anyone with a reasonable level of fitness. Never set out unless there is enough daylight to comfortably complete the route. Always wear appropriate footwear, especially as several of the paths may occasionally be boggy underfoot.

The guide is split into sections based on defined geographical areas, making it easier to explore from a fixed base. At the end of each section, there is a summary of useful local information. This includes public transport details, opening times of private gardens, phone numbers of trusts, Tourist Information Centres and youth hostels where available.

I truly enjoyed researching this guide and I wish you as much pleasure in discovering Cornwall for yourself. Finally, remember while enjoying these routes to leave only footprints and take only photographs.

## Acknowledgements

Thanks are due to the many people who helped me with this project by loaning me material, sharing their favourite parts of the county and even by walking the routes with me. My greatest debt of gratitude is to Andrew Dyer, without whom this book could not have been completed. Others who did sterling work as my protectors from bullocks and mad farm dogs include Steven Hagget, Stuart Seer, Graham Pratt and Ann-Marie Perring. Thanks also to Christine for the sandwiches and to Richard Horwood at the County Council Footpaths Division for his time and help, to Val Evans for getting all this started and to Terena Woods at Falmouth TIC and Anita James for the books and other information.


*Alexandra Pratt*

# Contents

## The North Coast

## The South Coast

## Bodmin Moor

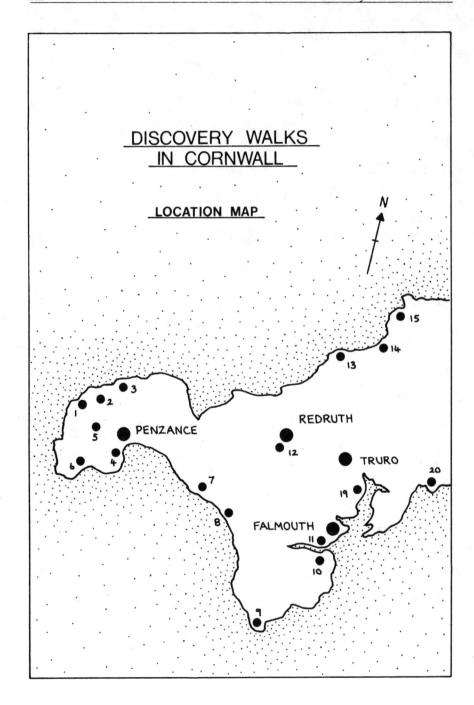

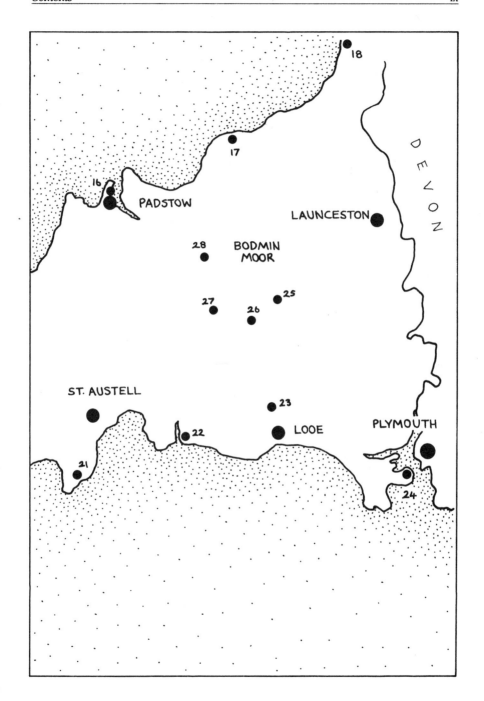

# The Far West, part 1:
# The Land's End Peninsula

*The Crowns mine: see walk 1*

# 1. Pendeen

**Route:**          Lighthouse – Levant Mine – Tregeseal Stone Circle –
                Carn Kenidjack – Pendeen Fogou – Lighthouse.

**Distance:**       7 miles

**Time:**           4 hours

**Terrain:**        Moderate. Mostly coastal and moorland walking.

**Refreshments:** Pendeen and Botallack

**Access:**         Pendeen Lighthouse is located on a minor road north of
                Pendeen, which is situated at the junction of the B3306
                and the B3318, north-east of St Just.

**Map:**            Ordnance Survey Explorer 7 Land's End. It is
                recommended that a map and a compass be taken when
                walking this route.

This route demonstrates the wealth and variety of this 'land of extremity'. From the cruel cliffs of the north coast to high, lonely moorland, the diversity of the natural landscape is matched only by the historic evidence of man's limited intervention here. The refurbished Levant mine explains the importance of tin and copper mining to Cornwall over the centuries, but such achievements are dwarfed by the mysterious and ancient Tregeseal Stone Circle and Pendeen Fogou, testaments to a time whose secrets were forgotten long ago.

The walk starts at Pendeen Lighthouse, which now belongs to the Trevithick Trust and is open to the public for a small admission price.

Go back along the road for a few metres until the path can be seen branching off to the cliffs on the right.

This first section has perhaps the most stunning views of the walk, as it follows the coastal path along a headland which faces the full might of the Atlantic. Care should be taken, however, as this landscape conceals a labyrinth of old mine workings, and only well-trodden paths are safe.

The first site on this walk is Geevor, one of three mines on this stretch of coast. Tin and copper mining have been an important aspect of Cornish life and economy since the Bronze Age. Indeed, part of this walk follows the ancient Tinners' Way, which dates from roughly 2000BC. This track was used

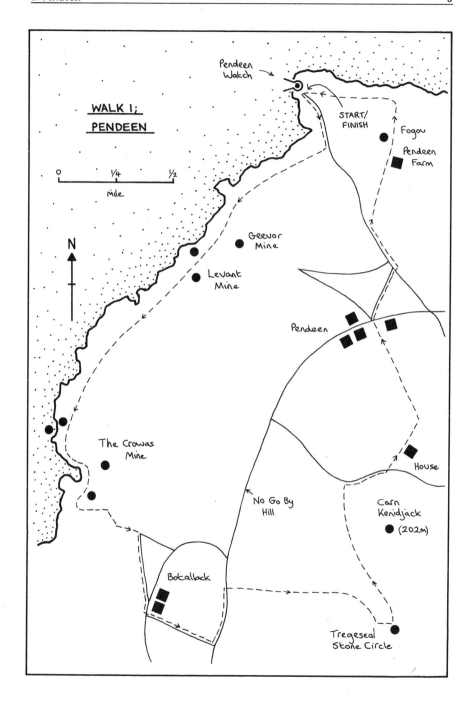

as a trade route for the transportation of precious metals down to the ports, from where they were sent as far afield as the Mediterranean. The remaining workings date from the 18th century onwards, with deep shaft mining, such as at Geevor, dating from the mid-19th century. This mine was one of the last to close, when the price of tin slumped in the 1980s. Many people here can tell of the sea turning bright green as far as half a mile out, and today the unnatural green and red colours of the rocks are reminders of the environmental realities of mining. Now, however, this site, like so many others in the area, is being refurbished, thus providing a new income from the old workings.

The next chimney on the horizon belongs to Levant Mine, which has been successfully refurbished and is open to the public. First opened in 1840, it was the scene of one of Cornwall's worst mining disasters, when in 1919 the main engine broke at the end of a shift, killing 31 men. The mine is now owned by the National Trust and includes a fully operational beam engine, used for pumping water out of the shafts.

From here the path continues past picturesque Botallack Mine, which exists in constant danger of being washed off its rocky outcrop, then turns left at the fork, following the wide track down to Manor Farm and Botallack village.

The village itself has little to offer, other than a cosy little pub, whose walls are covered with old photographs of the area. Don't be tempted to linger too long, however, as there is still a long way to go!

Take the St Just road south out of Botallack, then turn left down Truthwall Lane (follow the sign for the campsite). Go left at the junction, up No Go By Hill, then take the first right down the unsurfaced Kenthyon Lane. This section of the path is part of the Tinners' Way, easily identifiable as it leads up on to the high, undeveloped ground of Carnyorth Common. To reach Tregeseal Stone Circle, follow the yellow arrows to the far side of the water, then turn left and it is a few metres ahead on the right.

All the stone circles in this area have a certain hair-prickling atmosphere and Tregeseal is no exception, especially as its remote location ensures less visitors than say, the Merry Maidens, which are situated next to the B3315. At the foot of Carn Kenidjack (which is itself haunted by the Devil on a black horse), the 19 stones of Tregeseal form a true circle, the only survivor of a group of three on this site and now heavily restored. There are also two outlying cists to the north-east and several holed stones scattered about the common. Their purpose, like that of the stone circle, can only be guessed at.

Take the path in a north-westerly direction across the common, to the left of the carn, then turn right up the walled lane, emerging on Wheal Bal Hill. Turn right and walk along the road for a few minutes, then take the first left. Go right at the fork, past a farmhouse and along another walled trackway until the junction with a small lane which leads into Pendeen. Go left up this, then cross the main road. Ahead, on the opposite side of the main road, there is a fork. Take the road on the right, which crosses Calartha Common. At the junction turn left towards the coast. This road leads back to the lighthouse, but after about ten minutes there is short detour, taking the track on the right down to Pendeen House Farm. The fogou is on the north side of the farmyard. Ask at the farm for permission to view it.

*Fogous are as rare as they are unexplained. They are found only west of the River Fal in England, although there are similar passageways in Brittany and other Celtic areas. The Pendeen example has three passages, the longest of which is over 16 metres in length, although none are high enough for an adult to stand in. The fogou also includes a round chamber cut out of clay, unlike the passages, which are lined with stone. Opinion is divided as to their usage. Some think they were a refuge from raiders, others consider them as little more than storage spaces, or they could have been used for ritualistic purposes, although there is little evidence for this.*

From the fogou, the path back to Pendeen Watch is down the right-hand side of the field to the coastal path, then left up a final hill to the lighthouse.

# 2. Chun and The Nine Maidens

**Route:**    Rosemergy – Mên Scryfa – Nine Maidens Stone Circle –
Ding Dong Mine – Mên-An-Tol – Chun Castle (remains)
and Quoit – Iron Age Village – Rosemergy.

**Distance:**    6½ miles

**Time:**    3½ hours

**Terrain:**    Easy to moderate. Mostly moorland walking, with a few
relatively gentle climbs and some good views, both
coastal and inland.

**Refreshments:** None on route.

**Access:**    The small, informal car park at Rosemergy is next to the
mine shaft on the B3306, between Morvah and Treen. For
public transport details, see the useful information section.

**Map:**    Ordnance Survey Explorer 7 Land's End. It is
recommended that a compass be taken on this walk.

This walk covers both high ridges of moorland and the fearsome north coastline, which has claimed many an unwary ship. Much of the land is common land, whose ancient secrets remain locked in the stone circles, burial chambers and castles of its timeless landscape. With the exception of Ding Dong Mine, the monuments on this route all date from between the Bronze Age and the Dark Ages.

The path starts at Rosemergy car park, next to the mine stacks on the B3306. From here, turn right down the road for roughly 25 metres, then turn left at the green footpath sign. This path can be a little wet, but it soon climbs up the valley between Carn Galver and Watch Croft, Penwith's highest hill at 252 metres (760ft). Before cresting the summit, don't forget to turn around as there are some good views across both carns and down to the sea.

The path continues between stone walls, which border the traditionally small fields of West Penwith. Some date from the Iron Age, or even earlier – it's not only the monuments that tell of this area's ancient history. Just before the path opens out onto moorland, look to the right. Over the top of the walls the Bronze Age standing stone known as Mên Scryfa (from the Cornish meaning 'stone of writing') can be seen.

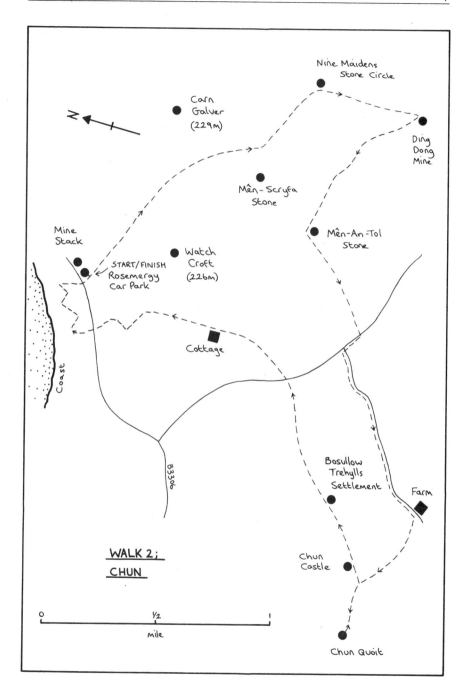

Nine Maidens
Stone Circle

Carn
Galver
(229m)

N

Ding
Dong
Mine

Mên-Scryfa
Stone

Mine
Stack

Mên-An-Tol
Stone

START/FINISH
Rosemergy
Car Park

Watch
Croft
(226m)

Coast

Cottage

B3306

Bosullow
Trehylls
Settlement

Farm

WALK 2;
CHUN

Chun
Castle

0        ½        1

mile

Chun Quoit

This stone is unusual in that it bears a Latin inscription dating from the early Dark Ages – written around a thousand years after the stone was erected. It reads RIALOBRAN CUNOVAL FIL, meaning 'Rialobran, son of Cunoval'. The latter was a chieftain whose son, legend has it, died fighting a usurper for the family land. The belief that he had been buried with treasures under the stone led to it being dug up in the 19th century, but it was later re-erected after several years of lying on the inscribed face (no treasure was ever reported as found).

As the path leaves the shelter of the stone walls, a choice of several paths across the moors presents itself. Take the route which continues directly up to the top of the ridge. From here, there are excellent views across the moorland in all directions. Beautiful as this can be, it can also be rather unpleasant in bad weather as there is no shelter and the path could easily be lost in poor visibility.

Don't confuse the ring of stones on the right with the Nine Maidens Stone Circle, which is a few minutes' walk further on. This first ring is not a circle, but the retaining stones of a barrow, usually part of Bronze Age burial chambers.

The stone circle proper is approximately 21 metres in diameter and has nine stones remaining upright, with another barrow on the south side. This was excavated in 1872 and was found to contain an urn and some pottery. This circle, also known as Boskednan, is one of only two true circles in the Penwith area. The other three are more elliptical, or flattened.

From the stone circle, face east and take the path on the right to Ding Dong Mine, which can clearly be seen on the horizon. This path has views across the moors down to Mount's Bay and St Michael's Mount itself.

The mine is thought to date from the early Dark Ages – which is quite young for an area which has been mined for four thousand years. The present remains belong to a mine which was opened in 1814, although the restored engine house dates from 1865. The mine shaft here reached a depth of 247 metres, although this is, of course, now capped.

From the mine, face north and take the path on the left, which goes north-west towards Watch Croft. This route leaves the windblown tops for lower, bracken-covered slopes. The path is well trodden though, and emerges at one of the most mysterious sites on the Land's End peninsula.

This is Men-An-Tol, a circular stone with a 51cm (20 inch) hole in the centre,

*Men-an-tol*

flanked by two upright stones. There are other hole-stones in the area, but none so large or regular as this. Such stones are thought to date from the Bronze Age, but like many things those people left behind, we have no explanation for their use. Legend has it that this stone, which is large enough for an adult to pass through, can cure certain illnesses and act as an oracle. This is achieved by placing two brass pins on the stone and observing whether they cross – thus rather limiting the range of its pronouncements!

The route continues past Men-An-Tol and over the stile to the track. Go left here and follow it until it emerges on the minor road at Bosullow (there is a phone box here, should it be needed). Take the lane on the opposite side of the road down to Trehylls Farm, where it ends. Here three paths strike out across Chun Downs. Take the middle one, which starts just to the left of the buildings on the right and leads straight up to the castle.

Chun Castle is an Iron Age hill fort dating from around 300BC. It must once have been truly formidable, built of two concentric walls, several metres thick and 85 metres in diameter. It was surrounded by a ditch and contained a clever staggered entrance, which would force any invaders to expose their undefended sides to attack from within the castle. It is very probable that the castle was highly significant in the tin trade as it is on the route known as the Tinners' Way, which runs from the mines of the St Just area to the port at Mounts Bay. This route would have been in use as early as the Bronze Age when the metalwork of the region was exported to Brittany, or even as far as the Mediterranean. Remains of a smelting furnace have been found in the castle (although nothing can be seen now), as has a 5½kg (12lb) lump of tin. It is thought that the castle was in use as late as the Dark Ages – thus occupied for almost one thousand years.

A few hundred metres to the west of the castle lies an even older monument to the building skills of our predecessors. Chun Quoit dates from around 3000BC, and is the best-preserved Neolithic chambered tomb in the region. The four slabs supporting the capstone remain upright to a height of one and three-quarter metres. Originally part of a barrow which was approximately 13½ metres in diameter, it was excavated in 1871 and it was discovered that the burial chamber itself had been rifled centuries before.

Retrace the path up to the castle and cross to the wall directly opposite the entrance. The continuation of the Tinners' Way lies north-east of here. A yellow arrow painted on a rock marks the start of the path, which can be difficult to find initially. The route goes down the hill for about 500 metres to the early Romano-British village of Bosullow Trehyllys. This is on private land (telephone 01736 261402 to view).

A little planning is worthwhile, however, as this is a good example of a courtyard settlement. The houses here are rectangular, some with walls up to one and three-quarter metres in height, with courtyards attached. Such a design is contrary to the Celtic Iron Age round house design. This 'courtyard' shape is Roman in origin although the Romans never made it this far west. Nevertheless, their influence can occasionally be seen. Around the settlement, the outline of tiny fields and paddocks can still be seen.

The path continues past the settlement, following the route of the Tinners' Way, which is marked by a slight depression in the ground and lined with boulders. It may become choked with bracken in high summer. This emerges on the lane which was crossed earlier, but slightly above Bosullow. Cross the road again and take the track directly opposite marked 'Mine Garden Cottage'. The path goes behind the cottage and downhill, passing a mine stack. There are good views of the northern coast before the path emerges on the B3306.

To avoid the short stretch of road up to the car park, turn right up the road for a few metres, then go left through the wooden gate marked with a footpath sign. the path goes down to the coast. Turn right through a single wooden gate and follow the path inland towards the mine stack and the car.

# 3. Zennor – an ancient landscape

**Route:**      Zennor Church – Zennor Quoit – Bishop's Head And Foot
– Mulfra Quoit – Bodrifty Iron Age Settlement –
Bosporthennis Quoit – Gurnard's Head – Chapel Jane –
Zennor.

**Distance:**    8½ miles

**Time:**    4¼ hours

**Terrain:**    Moderate to challenging. Mostly moorland, with some
coastal walking. Some steep climbs and little-used paths.

**Refreshments:** Zennor only

**Access:**    Limited car parking at Zennor, on the B3306, west of St
Ives. If using public transport, see end of chapter for
details.

**Map:**    Ordnance Survey Explorer 7, Land's End. It is highly
recommended that a map and compass are used when
walking this route.

Set at the foot of the moors of West Penwith on the unforgiving north coast, Zennor is an attractive but tiny hamlet. It grew out of farming and mining, both a feature of this area since prehistory, a time whose presence is very strong here thanks to the large number of ancient monuments still standing. Even the tiny, stone-edged fields surrounding the village date from the Bronze Age, and it is likely that tin streaming in the valley dates from the same period. Every footstep of this walk is steeped in history. It also visits some of the wildest parts of this area, including the only significant moorland west of Bodmin, as well as the equally dramatic north coast cliffs.

The small but indomitable stone church of St Senara presides over Zennor. Legend links her to Princess Asenara of Brittany who was nailed in a barrel at some time in the 6th century and thrown into the sea. She was, however, saved by an angel and went on to found several parishes, including Zennor. As usual, such stories contain a modicum of truth. Senara was most probably one of the many missionaries who travelled in the remaining Celtic lands of the west, including Ireland and Brittany, during the Dark Ages.

The present church dates from the 12th century and holds many things of interest, not least the ceiling. Its unusual barrel vaulting is relatively common in Cornwall and is reminiscent of a ship's keel. The churchyard contains three cross heads. The cross at the main entrance is wheel-headed, with a Latin cross on the front and back. The other two are by a grave and both have unusual representations of the Christ figure carved on one side. They were originally used as wayside crosses on the path from St Ives to Zennor.

However, by far the most unusual thing in the church is the mermaid bench end. Carved around five hundred years ago, the symbolism it contains is pre-Christian. Mermaids were used to represent Aphrodite, goddess of sea and love. Christianity used the dual nature of the mermaid to represent the two natures of Christ – God and man. Legend states that this particular mermaid lured a local chorister to his death in the sea at nearby Pendour Cove and an attentive ear can hear the lovers singing on a summer's eve.

D.H. Lawrence loved the place so much he came to live here with his German wife, Frieda, during the First World War. Lawrence was a regular at the Tinners' Arms, below the church, and much of *Women In Love* was written here. However, the paranoia of war led the local people to believe that the couple were German spies and so they hounded them out of the village. This experience later became the basis for an episode in one of his novels.

There are two roads into and out of the village, but car drivers can use only one route. It is clearly signed and the walk also uses this route. It is the shorter road, which passes the water pump, and after a few hundred metres emerges onto the B3306. Turn right here, then turn left down a track just before the stone bridge. Before the track becomes a path, there is a small sign next to a stone stile on the left marked 'Quoit' (this may be removed in winter months). Cross this and follow the path up the hill, passing the Logan Stone on the right and rounding The Carne.

From this unusual rock formation there are excellent views across the moors and the sweep of tiny, walled fields down to the sea.

Take the path around to the other side of the summit, heading south-east to Zennor Quoit, which is on the right of the path.

This is one of the largest and, despite the damage, one of the most impressive Neolithic quoits (or burial chambers) in the area. The capstone is 5½ metres long and weighs about 9½ tonnes. It would originally have been set within a barrow almost 4 metres in diameter, although nothing of that remains now. Dr Borlase saw the monument in its entirety in the mid-18th

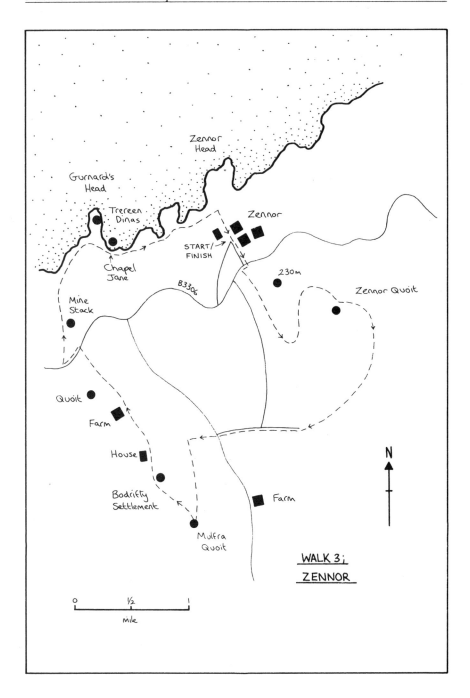

Zennor Head

Gurnard's Head

Treseen Dinas

Zennor

START/FINISH

Chapel Jane

B3306

230m

Zennor Quoit

Mine Stack

Quoit

Farm

House

Bodrifty Settlement

Farm

Mulfra Quoit

N

WALK 3;
ZENNOR

0      ½      1
mile

century, but it suffered extensive damage by a local farmer in the following century, before he could be bribed to stop by a member of the Borlase family. Legend has it that the quoit was the 'table' at which Arthur dined with local rulers before going into battle against the Danes who had landed at Gwynver Beach. The latter were, of course, routed by Arthur and his followers.

**At the first junction in the path after the quoit, go right.**

This is the intersection of two ancient trackways dating from the Bronze Age or even earlier.

**Continue down the path, going south, past the sign to Embla Vean on the left. At the next junction in the path, go right. This becomes a track, which emerges at the oddly named Bishop's Head And Foot.**

This square stone in the ground in the middle of the track marks where the three parishes of Zennor, Gulval and Trowednack meet. The place was marked by a cross, although that was lost some time in the past three centuries.

**Continue up the road to the T-junction. Opposite there is a small parking place for cars. A few feet to the left of this, by the telegraph pole, is a path**

*Mulfra Quoit*

which strikes straight up to the moors. Take this until it reaches a cross-roads in paths. Turn left, ascending the hill, and the path will eventually reach the quoit.

Mulfra is another Neolithic chamber tomb. Like Zennor, it has not survived 5000 years without some damage. Happily though, in this case there is slightly less. Mulfra Quoit stands 1¾ metres high, although the capstone has slipped, as did that at Lanyon Quoit, possibly during a thunderstorm in the 18th century. Borlase excavated it and found 'soils' of various colours, which were probably ritualistic in origin. There are excellent views from the top of the hill and, on all but the worst days, St Michael's Mount can be seen.

This is as far as the route goes towards the south coast, however, as the path leaves the summit on the west side, then swings to the right and goes north-west around the base (do not continue on the main path straight down to the west). Cross a stone stile into a large field which contains Bodrifty Settlement.

This settlement dates from the Bronze Age, with evidence of later habitation during the Iron Age. Its only defence appears to have been an earth bank, which is now only just less than a metre in height. The site contains seven easily discernible huts, although there were probably more. Some have fairly high walls, and the layout of the village is not difficult to envisage. It was excavated in the 1950s, revealing a large quantity of pottery, internal drains and paved walkways. To the east are the remains of a field system, although this is difficult to see, mainly due to the rampant growth of gorse and bracken.

Leave the settlement over the stile onto the track to the west, then go left through the metal gate. Turn right up the track, heading towards the cottage on the opposite slope. The path goes in front of the cottage before going onto open moorland from the far (north) side of the field in front of the house. This path then weaves between fields to reach Bosporthennis Farm and the path next to the stream. Turn left here, going north, with the stream on the right. A few hundred metres away is the site of Bosporthennis Quoit. After the last farm building on the left, next to the metal hay rack, go diagonally uphill through three fields. The quoit lies in the fourth field, bounded by high, stone walls, which can make it very hard to find.

The surrounding barrow of the quoit (unlike Mulfra and Zennor) can still be seen and measures 6 metres across. Three of the four uprights are still in place, but the capstone lies on the ground inside. The curious shape of this is the result of the labours of an enterprising miller, before he decided against using it as a millstone. There are also some good views here down the valley to the sea.

Return to the path and follow the stream through the empty gateways of fields, until you reach a field with a stile about 20 metres in from the water. The step on the approaching side is small, but the next field is much lower. Follow the path, crossing stiles, until reaching the fork, just before some trees. Go right and cross the stream, then continue down to the road (this little section is often boggy). Turn left up the road and go over the bridge. Round the corner and on the right is a well-trodden path. Go down through the trees to a stile. This leads down to the coast, passing a mine stack on the way. Once on the coastal path, turn right, towards Zennor.

Approximately three-quarters of a mile along the coastal path is the unmistakable promontory of Gurnard's Head. This is the site of an Iron Age cliff castle. For something so old, a surprising amount can still be seen. Across the neck of the promontory there are ditches and ramparts 60 metres long, with a staggered entrance in the centre. Some of the ramparts are almost 2 metres in height, protecting a settlement represented now by the traces of 16 circular huts which can still be found. On the east side of the promontory, at the base, there is a small, early Medieval chapel called Chapel Jane built into the side of the cliff beside the footpath down to Treen Cove. It can be difficult to see as the remains of the walls are surrounded by bracken and other undergrowth. The remains can only just be seen, as can the altar which lies nearby. The unusual name comes from the Cornish 'yeyn', meaning 'bleak', or 'cold', which this exposed corner of the coast can certainly be on all but the finest days.

From here, it is an exhilarating walk back across the cliffs to Zennor Head, although this can be quite close to the edge in places and should not be attempted in mist. On the western base of the promontory, after the footbridge, there is a small lane on the right which goes up to the village, where the Tinners' Arms can provide a well-earned reward!

# 4. Mousehole and Lamorna

**Route:** Mousehole – Castallack Round and Stone – The Pipers – Merry Maidens Stone Circle- Tregiffian Barrow – Lamorna – Kemyel Crease Reserve – Mousehole.

**Distance:** 6¼ miles

**Time:** 3 hours

**Terrain:** Moderate. Includes some steep stretches of coastal path.

**Refreshments:** Mousehole and Lamorna

**Access:** Mousehole is 1½ miles around the bay from Newlyn, and a short bus ride from Penzance bus and train stations.

**Maps:** Ordnance Survey Explorer 7 Land's End and Ordnance Survey Landranger 203.

Pronounced locally as 'Mouzel' this village is reputed to be the prettiest in Cornwall. The pilchard fishing around which the village grew died out fifty years ago, although Mousehole is still a working harbour. Outside the harbour walls lies Merlin's Rock, which features in a prophecy made by the seer himself:

> 'There shall land on the Rock Of Merlin
> Those That Shall Burn Paul, Penzance And Newlyn.'

Astonishingly, this is exactly what happened in 1595, when the Spanish invaded and burnt all but the manor house (now the Keigwin Arms) to the ground. The area is also famous as the resting place, a mile inland at Paul, of Dolly Pentreath, the last native Cornish speaker, who died in 1777. Despite the decline of fishing, life and the sea are still closely interwoven in the far west. In 1981 the local lifeboat, *Solomon Browne*, was lost with all hands whilst trying to rescue a coaster. Even now, life can be lost to the vagaries of the ocean.

Leave the village via the footpath which is clearly marked on the south side of the chapel, situated just above the southern end of the harbour. This leads straight uphill to a lane. Go right for a few metres, then turn left up a flight of stone steps into a field.

Don't forget to look back as the views of Mousehole and across the bay to the Mount are amongst the best in this entire area.

From here, follow the footpath past Halwyn Farm, crossing five fields. The first two stiles are in the far corners of the fields, but in the third there is something of a crossroads. Keep to the hedge on the right and cross the stile in the corner into a large, irregular field. The other two stiles are in the opposite hedges, in a diagonal line to the right and the road.

On reaching the lane turn right, then left at the T-junction. This lane goes to Castallack and the footpath follows the same route, but on the other side of the hedge on the right. It is clearly marked. Return to the road just before Castallack and go past the large, modern barn on the right, by its gable end, and then turn right through the wooden gate. Go past the house and down the grassy lane. This is probably very old as it leads to Castallack Round. Look out for a narrow path through the grass on the right after the old lane has become a path, about 230 metres after leaving Castallack.

The Round is a circular field, with parts of the wall remaining up to six feet high. Rounds are Iron Age settlements with less defences than hill forts, usually just a single wall and ditch to protect the homestead. Just to the north-west of this and a little further along the path are the remains of a hut circle. To the west by a few metres (again, follow the little paths) is a Bronze Age standing stone, just under two metres in height.

On returning to the main path, it widens once again and winds downhill into the almost perfect valley of Lamorna.

There are some excellent views, inland this time, from this part of the path.

The lane emerges on to the B3315. Turn left and follow it until it climbs a hill. This ancient hamlet is called Trewoofe.

There are several legends in this area which link the once powerful Lovelis family with the Devil, who is usually portrayed as riding a black horse. The Rosemerryn fogou is still said to be haunted by Squire Lovelis's tormented spirit. On an equally cheerful note, the next hill leads to a 'place of slaughter', otherwise known as Boleigh, which was the site of the last battle between the Cornish and English in AD935, completing King Athelstan's conquest of the West.

This fogou is possibly the most unusual of these highly mysterious monuments. Built during the Iron Age, they are underground passageways, often branching, or opening out into a room (such as Carn Euny, near Sancreed).

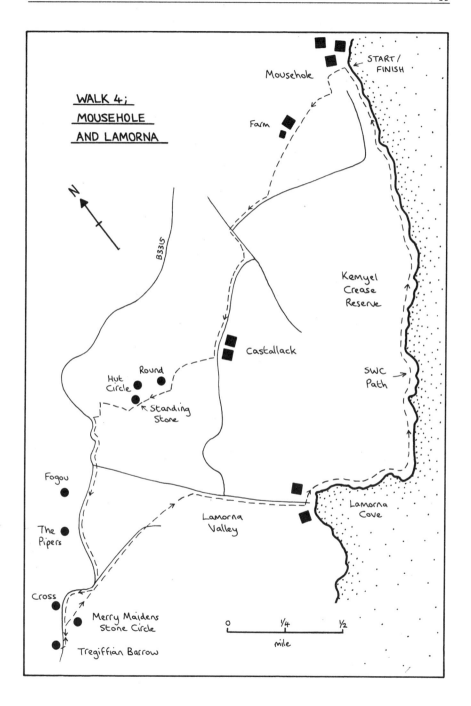

WALK 4;
MOUSEHOLE
AND LAMORNA

START /
FINISH

Mousehole

Farm

N

B3315

Kemyel
Crease
Reserve

Castallack

SWC
Path

Round
Hut
Circle
Standing
Stone

Fogou

Lamorna
Cove

The
Pipers

Lamorna
Valley

Cross

Merry Maidens
Stone Circle

Tregiffian Barrow

0     ¼     ½

mile

The word 'fogou' comes from the Cornish for cave. It is thought they served one of three functions: a refuge from raiders, a storage area, or as a place of worship. Rosemerryn gives the strongest evidence for the latter theory. It contains a carving of a human torso and head. This is the only known Iron Age carving in the county, and is thought to represent a Celtic god. It is on private property, however, so ask for permission to view at the house across the stream at the end of the second track on the right after Trewoofe.

**Once over the hill at Boleigh, the Pipers can clearly be seen. They are set back a little from the road, but are easily accessed.**

The tallest of the two is 15ft (5 metres) high; the other 13½ft (4.5 metres). Thought to be Bronze Age in origin (during which time this area was densely populated), they may have acted as wayside markers or territorial boundary stones. They may also simply be part of a system of outlying monuments connected to the Merry Maidens stone circle, which lies four hundred metres to the south-west.

**To reach this, follow the first footpath sign for the circle, at the bend in the road, and go across a field.**

This is a very well-known and often visited site (perhaps because of its location). The nineteen stones form a true circle 26 metres (78ft) in diameter which was probably used for public ceremonies and rituals. The legend of the schoolgirls caught dancing on a Sunday and turned to stone, along with their musicians (the Pipers), probably dates from as late as the 18th century, though is possibly of pagan origin.

**Leave the circle through the wooden stile in the western corner and turn left down the road. A few metres further on is Tregiffian Barrow.**

This is a Neolithic chambered tomb dating from around 4000 BC. It is 3.5 metres (14ft) long. Amazingly, the road goes over part of it, despite the fact that it is a national monument. It was excavated in 1871 and an unusual carved stone was found (now placed in Truro Museum and replaced by a replica). On the floor were bones, charcoal and some urns containing human remains.

**Retrace the route back to the stile at which you left the B road (at the sign for the stone circle). Instead of walking up the road; however, turn right along the road marked as a dead end, past the rest home. Just before the fork, there is also a Wesleyan chapel on the right.**

Wesleyanism came to Cornwall in the early 18th century, against a back-

*The author at 'The Pipers', Boleigh*

ground of poor representation, corruption and poverty, issues the bureau-cratic Anglican Church found difficult to combat, especially in the face of changing population patterns. Wesley appealed mainly to the working classes, mostly miners and fishermen. By 1781, up to 20 000 people at a time would come to hear Wesley speak at Gwennap Pit near Redruth. One of the reasons for the growth of the New Dissent was the building of many small chapels such as the one at Trewoofe, which could serve the need of ru-ral, isolated communities, often neglected by Anglican ministers.

**Take the left fork and continue straight on along the bridle path sign-posted for Lamorna. At the road, go right and walk down into the cove.**

Lamorna is famously the home of the writer Derek Tangye. The nearby cliffs were also the meeting place of a middle-aged Marconi and a local girl, Betty Paynter, who became the love of his life.

**From the quay, walk in front of the terraced cottages and cross the stream. The route goes up the side of the valley. Take the path on the right marked as the coastal path.**

The walk along the cliffs back to Mousehole is as pretty a walk as anyone could wish for, especially in spring, when the clifftops are bright with the pinks, yellows and purples of wild flowers and busy with birds building nests. The only steep sections are at either end, and much of the middle section is barely above the ocean.

Approximately halfway along this coastal section is a small nature reserve, Kemyel Crease, owned by the Cornish Wildlife Trust. Bought in 1974, this plantation occupies small fields known as quillets. The most prominent spe-cies are Monterey pine, Lawson's cypress and Scots pine. The coniferous trees provide shelter for native broadleaved tress and shrubs, many of which were planted after the storms of the late 1980s. Amongst the more common ferns is the occasional patch of white ramping -fumitory, which is of local interest.

**As the path nears Mousehole, it becomes a track and passes some houses. At the junction with the road down into the village, turn right and follow the steep road down past the bird sanctuary on the left. This was first opened in 1928 and is now run by the RSPCA. Visitors are welcome, for a small donation. The harbour and the village centre are directly ahead.**

# 5. Carn Euny and Boscawen-un

**Route:**       Sancreed Church and Crosses – Chapel Downs Holy Well
– Sancreed Beacon – Carn Euny Settlement – Chapel
Carn Brea – Crows-An-Wra – Boscawen-Un Stone Circle
– Sancreed.

**Distance:**    6¾ miles (shorter route – 4¼ miles)

**Time:**        3½ hours (shorter route – 2¼ hours)

**Terrain:**     Easy to moderate. Moorland and farmland. Some of the
fields may contain cattle, so keep dogs on a lead.

**Refreshments:** None on the route.

**Access:**      To reach Sancreed by car, turn right at Drift, on the A30
west of Penzance, and follow the signs. For public
transport information, see end of chapter.

**Maps:**        Ordnance Survey Explorer 7 Land's End.

This walk is right at the heart of Penwith, both geographically and
historically. It follows a route which is 4000 years old in places, and
will uncover sites dating from the Bronze Age to the Dark Ages. It includes the Iron Age settlement of Carn Euny, which is one of the best
examples of its kind in the area and whose curious underground
passageway is still largely intact, and the highly atmospheric
Boscawen-un Stone Circle. The walk can be shortened by missing
out Chapel Carn Brea and details of the short cut are in the text.
Don't forget your camera!

The tiny hamlet of Sancreed is situated in the only parish in the area without a coastline. It has a lovely church, which dates from the 15th century, although there are two of the best late Dark Age stone crosses in Cornwall in
the churchyard. The one on the south porch is inscribed with the sculptor's
own name 'Runho' and the shaft has double knotwork. The other cross is inscribed 'INCX X· with designs on all four sides, including a vase and flower.

Many churches in Cornwall are built on or near to the cells of early saints or
hermits. These were, in turn, located by holy wells, which often have a Chris-

tian superstructure but pre-Christian powers. Chapel Downs Holy Well is a good example of this.

The well is a few minutes' walk from the village (follow the signs opposite the church, passing the concrete hut). There is a tiny ruined chapel next to it and a modern cross.

The tree overhanging the well is adorned with rags and other offerings. This is an ancient custom which is believed to invoke the well's healing and prophetic powers – its modern miracles will be vigorously attested to by local people today.

Retrace the path to the church and turn left, then left again, uphill to Sancreed Beacon. At the summit, on the right, there is a wooden gate onto the Beacon.

At 525ft (172 metres), this offers some of the best views in West Cornwall, rivalled only by Chapel Carn Brea. The Beacon is owned by the Cornwall Heritage Trust. It is a nature reserve and is a particularly good place to see birds of prey. The reserve is also the site of a Bronze Age settlement, the outline of which can still be seen, as can the remains of a field system and a burial mound.

*Holy well, Carn Euny*

Five minutes further down the road there is a left turn on to a bridleway, just before the first buildings of Grumbla. Follow this until it forms a T-junction with a wider track. Turn left and then left again, following the signs for Carn Euny along a path past the back of a house on the left.

Carn Euny was discovered by a miner in the 19th century and was excavated in 1928. Occupied periodically throughout the Iron Age, it has an excellent mixture of round and courtyard houses. However, its most notable feature is the 18-metre long fogou (meaning cave in Cornish), or souterrain. Comparable to those

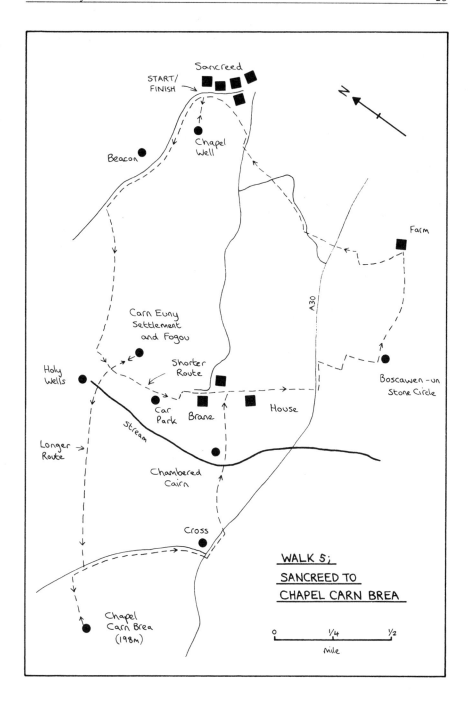

Sancreed

START/
FINISH

N

Beacon

Chapel
Well

Farm

Carn Euny
Settlement
and Fogou

A30

Holy
Wells

Shorter
Route

Car
Park

Brane

House

Boscawen-un
Stone Circle

Longer
Route

Stream

Chambered
Cairn

Cross

WALK 5;
SANCREED TO
CHAPEL CARN BREA

Chapel
Carn Brea
(198m)

0      ¼      ½

mile

in Brittany, it has a side passage leading to an intact circular chamber containing a mysterious, flueless fireplace. It is still unclear as to what the fogous were used for. Opinion is divided as to whether they were for religious purposes, as a cold storage, or as a refuge from raiders.

The shorter route retraces the path to the lane and goes left, down into the hamlet of Brane. Follow the road through the hamlet, turning right at the T-junction and then going straight on, continuing down a track as the road swings 90 degrees to the left. This emerges at a junction in footpaths – and is where the longer route emerges after Brane Barrow.

The longer route entails leaving the settlement by the same entrance, and turning right then taking the first left down to Chapel Euny Holy Well.

This well, like the one near Sancreed, originally had a small chapel next to it, although that has now been lost. The well itself has several steps descending into its cool darkness, with two worked stones at the entrance. Like most similar wells, it has healing powers, although these appear to be active only on the first three Wednesdays of May.

Continue along this path, crossing Tredinney Common, before emerging on a minor road. Cross this to the small gravel car park and go through the kissing gate, following the path to the summit.

The views from here are stunning, stretching in every direction and taking in the huge expanse of the Atlantic and the hills and moorland to the north and away to the east. The massive white satellite dishes at Goonhilly Earth Station on the Lizard Peninsula can just be seen on a clear day. Also at the summit are the remains of two Bronze Age barrows and a medieval chapel. It is the site of the first in a chain of bonfires to be lit across Cornwall on Midsummer's Eve. Members of the St Just Old Cornwall Society sing and pray in Cornish whilst sacrificing herbs and flowers to the sun god.

Return to the road, turn right and proceed to Crows-an-Wra, marked by a Celtic Cross.

This unusual name means 'Witch's Hill' and was named after a hermit who lived in the chapel on Carn Brea and was accused of being a sorcerer by the Dean of St Buryan.

Turn left along the A30 and a few metres along the road, in the direction of Penzance, there is a footpath sign on the left. Follow this across three fields, keeping the hedge on the right. It then becomes a walled track which goes through Cardinney Farm. At the end of their driveway, cross the track and continue on, going down the side of the house at the crossroads. This section of the path is part of the ancient Tinners' Way, which dates from the Bronze Age or even earlier and was used to transport tin and copper from the mines in the St Just area down to the port at St Michael's Mount, from where they sent on to Brittany and beyond.

The route passes the magnificent Brane Barrow, a well-preserved Scillonian chamber tomb from the Neolithic period which is 6 metres in diameter and 2 metres tall. The barrow is on private land, but can be seen on the left from the footpath, or better still, from the top of the large stile found just after crossing the stream.

After going through a large iron gate, there is a junction of paths and the two routes join.

Turn right (or, if approaching from Brane, continue straight) down the overgrown lane and proceed to a T-junction – there is a house on the right. Turn right and cross the stile on the left at the top of the driveway to the house. Continue across six fields, all of which have stone stiles, until the road is reached. Turn left and continue until a small, wooden gate can be seen on the right. Go down through the gorse until the path forks. Here, go through the small gate on the left and follow the path until it emerges at the well-hidden Boscawen-un Stone Circle

This is the most complete and possibly the most significant circle in West Penwith. It certainly has an atmosphere which is missing from more popular sites. Each of the stones is granite, except one which is pure quartz. The central stone leans towards two stone slabs, possibly cists, which lie on the outside of the circle. It was most likely in use up to the Dark Ages as a site of the Gorsedd of the Island of Britain – an event revived by Druid Henry Jenner in 1928. The Gorsedd is now held annually at different sites around Cornwall, including Boscawen-un.

Exit on the east side of the circle, 90 degrees clockwise from the entry point. Follow the narrow, hedged path to Boscawen Farm, then turn left down the track, passing a standing stone in the hedge on the left. Cross the A30 and follow the public footpath signs across two fields, emerging on a lane next to the building. Turn right and go through the hamlet of Tregonbris until you reach the second footpath sign, which points straight on as the road swings to the right. This again crosses two fields, keeping the hedge first on the left, then on the right. Turn left along the lane, then right at the sign, keeping the hedge on the right. Go right along the lane to the next sign on the left, which leads down into Sancreed, seen clearly ahead.

# 6. Smuggling Country –
# Porthgwarra to Penberth

**Route:**        Porthgwarra – Porth Chapel – Minack Theatre – Museum
                 of Submarine Telegraphy – Porthcurno – Treryn Dinas
                 Fort (remains) – Penberth – St Levan Church, Stone and
                 Crosses – Porthgwarra.

**Distance:**     5½ miles (shorter route – 4¼ miles)

**Time:**         3 hours (shorter route – 2 hours)

**Terrain:**      Moderate, with some steep coastal sections unsuitable for
                 very small children.

**Refreshments:** Porthgwarra during the summer months, and Porthcurno.

**Access:**       Car parks at Porthgwarra (turn off the B3315 at Polgigga)
                 £1 per day and  at Treen, 60 pence per day (summer
                 charges only). Buses from Penzance, see end of chapter
                 for details.

**Maps:**         Ordnance Survey Explorer 7 Land's End or Ordnance
                 Survey Landranger 103.

This is my favourite walk on the Land's End Peninsula as it combines stunning scenery with layers of myth and legend. There are
also plenty of things to explore along the way, including smugglers'
caves, Celtic crosses, an ancient cliff castle, three excellent beaches
and a unique open air theatre. Much of the walk is coastal, offering
some of the best sea views in Britain, especially when the cliffs are
full of flowers and there is a good chance of seeing a school of dol-
phins playing just offshore.

The walk starts in Porthgwarra but if public transport is used, Treen or
Porthcurno may be more convenient starting places.

The lane down to the cove from the B3315 is narrow and twists between high
hedges which border farming land. It comes as a shock then, when the landscape suddenly opens out into a swathe of moorland which sweeps down to
the ocean and is coloured purple, yellow, pink and a brilliant green in the summertime.

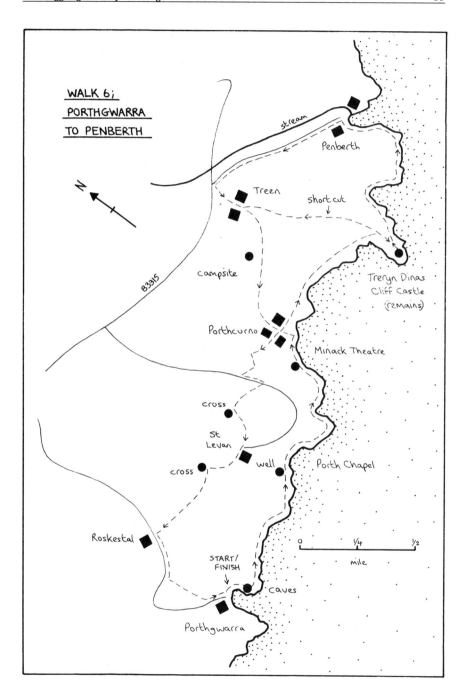

WALK 6;
PORTHGWARRA
TO PENBERTH

N

stream

Penberth

Treen

short cut

B3315

campsite

Treryn Dinas
Cliff Castle
(remains)

Porthcurno

Minack Theatre

cross

St
Levan

cross

well

Porth Chapel

Roskestal

START/
FINISH

Caves

Porthgwarra

0        1/4       1/2

mile

The cove itself has a small scattering of houses, an even smaller beach and some wonderful, natural tunnels through the cliffs, which will delight children and adults alike. These caves, like the rest of this section of coast, were the scene of much smuggling in the 18th and 19th centuries. Porthgwarra was the haunt of so-called 'gentlemen smugglers', who brought contraband brandy in from France, using their social standing as a cover for their illegal activities. However, it was not only men who were involved in this dangerous, but profitable business, as the ballad 'The Female Smuggler' tells. One such woman was Martha Blewett who smuggled salt, and was murdered not far from the cove in 1792.

The path leads up the left side of the cove, going east between the two nearest cottages. Follow the signs to the right, up through the green tunnel to the top of the cliff. The path along the coast is clearly marked and is a beautiful walk on a clear day. In early summer, the cliffs are pink, blue and yellow with wild flowers.

The first cove on the route is that of Porth Chapel. The holy well of St Selevan is on the path at the top of the cliff, and the water is still used for baptisms in the nearby church of St Levan. Part-way down the steps to the beach, on the left side, are the remains of the chapel, which dates from the 8th century. At the base of the steps there is a short scramble to the beach, which has beautiful golden sand, but is not very suitable for swimming.

Continue along the cliff path until it emerges at the car park for the Minack Theatre. From here, go to the opposite side where there is a choice of three routes. The two on the right lead down into the Minack.

This amazing open air theatre is carved into the side of the cliff and looks like half an old Roman amphitheatre. It is hard to believe that it was the life's work of one woman, Rowena Cade. She started work on it with the help of her gardener in 1932, after several successful open air productions in a local wooded dell. It is hard to imagine a better backdrop for a performance than the evening sun dying on the cliffs opposite, then the moon rising above the ocean, just beyond the stage. The theatre and small museum can be visited during the day (except during matinées) and there are evening performances from May to September. The theatre is closed during the winter months.

The route continues down the left path at the choice of three and goes down a very steep cliff onto the beach at Porthcurno.

This is a much larger beach than the previous two and is very popular in the

*Celtic cross and packhorse stone*

summertime. There is a lifeguard here in the summer months, so it is safe to swim (unless the lifeguard flags indicate otherwise). A few hundred metres up the valley from the head of the beach, a large white building can be seen on the right. This is owned by the Trevithick Trust and houses an underground Museum of Submarine Telegraphy which offers guided tours. It is worth a visit and is open every day except Saturday from 10am to 4pm.

The path continues on up to the left of the beach, past the museum building. Follow the yellow arrow at the gate. There is another pleasant stretch of coastal path up to Treryn Dinas Fort and the Logan Rock.

This promontory is directly opposite the Minack Theatre, and on clear days the distant sound of applause can be heard after a matinée. The path splits three ways at this point. Go right to explore the promontory, which is the site of an Iron Age cliff castle. There are four lines of defence, which include ditches and ramparts up to 274 metres long at the neck of the promontory, and the rest is naturally defended from the sea by the vertical cliffs and jagged rocks. The fort is thought to have been occupied from the third to the first centuries BC, and remains unexcavated. This is not to say the castle doesn't have a colourful history. There are many legends surrounding the site, which involve 'small people', witches and a giant who is said to have murdered his wife, thereby turning her into the 'Lady Logan'.

The Logan Rock is perched at the very summit of the natural rock formations. Like several in Cornwall, it could be rocked by a small pressure, despite its immense size. Merlin prophesied that that when the 'key' (i.e. the rock) was removed, the castle would sink beneath the waves. This, unlike some of his other pronouncements, did not happen, however, when Oliver Goldsmith's nephew removed it for a joke in 1824. He was forced to replace it at his own expense and it still moves, although only with a good deal of effort. This is not the only legend to connect Arthur to the castle. Even though he lived some time after the fort was occupied, it is thought to have been in his possession and Merlin is said to be magically imprisoned forever in a cave beneath the rock.

To reach Treen and thereby shorten the route, go back to the split in the path and go inland at the National Trust obelisk. The village is about 10 minutes away. I recommend, however, walking an extra mile and including the small cove of Penberth. Continue straight on along the coastal path, past the castle.

The path soon descends into a tiny but truly picturesque harbour at the end of a valley which is rich, fertile and filled with flowers in late spring and early summer. There is a small stream running the length of the valley, which can be crossed via an ancient stone bridge at the head of the harbour. Penberth was given to the National Trust in the 1950s in memory of those killed in the Second World War.

Follow the lane up Penberth valley to the road. Treen village can be seen up on the left, a few metres away.

The pub is one of the first buildings on the right and a more perfect example of a West Country hostelry would be difficult to find.

From Treen, take the track opposite the village shop down to the camp-site. Go into the first field, passing the toilet block. The stile is in the middle of the left (south facing) wall. The next is in the far corner to the right. Follow the line of stiles across five fields (they follow a straight line in a south-westerly direction) until the route emerges on a sandy track in Porthcurno valley. Go left, then take the first right (following the sign for the beach café). Once on the road, turn left, then turn right behind the large, white hotel on the corner and walk down into the hamlet of Rospletha. At the far end of the houses, go through the kissing gate on the left and into fields. The path is clear straight across to the spire of St Levan church, which can be seen in the distance.

The path goes straight past a Celtic cross. This is one of four crosses placed around the church of St Levan to ward off pagan influences. St Levan was one of the many Irish saints who came to Britain in the Dark Ages and spread Christianity amongst the people. There are two more stone crosses in the churchyard, plus something a little less holy. In the graveyard, near the entrance to the church, is a cleft stone. Legend has it that Arthur and Merlin visited the site, and on seeing the rock Merlin announced, 'When a pack horse can pass through it, the world will be done.' It may be a comfort to know that the cleft is still less than one foot wide.

The route continues past the footpath sign in the turning space opposite the churchyard. It leads up into fields once again. Follow the path over the stile and at the stone cross, turn left, aiming for a stile in the opposite wall. From here, a walled track down into the village of Rosketsal can be seen. Go through the hamlet and on to the road. Turn left, then continue straight on at the footpath sign as the road takes a sharp right. This track leads down into Porthgwarra. As the path reaches a white house on the right, take a hairpin right down the side of the house, and back into the cove.

# Useful Information

**Transport in the Penwith Area:** Using public transport to get around the peninsula, particularly the more remote areas, may be quite a challenge. There are excellent train services to the main line station at Penzance, although this is, unfortunately, the last station on the line. All rail enquires: 0345 484950. The train station and the main bus station in Penzance are located next to each other at the bottom of Market Jew Street. For telephone enquires regarding local services, phone 01209 719988.

For services to the Isles of Scilly from Penzance via ferry or helicopter, call 0345 105555.

**Other Information:** Trevithick Trust (Walks 1 and 6) – (Porthcurno) 01736 810966, (Pendeen) 01735 788418, (Geevor) 01735 788662. Minack Theatre (Walk 6) – 01736 810181, Levant Mine (National Trust) (Walk 1) – 01736 786156, St Michael's Mount (National Trust) – 01736 710507, National Trust Regional Office 01208 74281.

**Tourist Information Offices:** Penzance, Station Road – 01736 362207, St Ives, The Guildhall, Street-An-Pol 01736 796297.

**Youth hostels:** Castle Horneck, Penzance 01736 362666, Letcha Vean, St Just 01736 788437.

# The Far West, part 2: The Lizard Peninsula and Redruth

*Porthleven Beach: see walk 8*

# 7. Germoe and Tregonning Hill

**Route:**            Germoe Church and Well – Godolphin House – Castle
                     Pencaire (remains) – Tregonning Hill – Germoe.

**Distance:**         5 miles

**Time:**             2½ hours

**Terrain:**          Moderate. Mostly farmland and moorland, with some hills.

**Refreshments:** Godolphin village (on route)

**Access:**           Germoe is situated a quarter of a mile from the A394,
                     between Helston and Penzance. If travelling by bus, take
                     the Helston to Penzance service and get off at Praa
                     Sands, then walk up to Germoe.

**Map:**              Ordnance Survey Explorer 7 Land's End.

This walk visits a variety of sites in a part of the county often neglected in favour of more dramatic seascapes or greater expanses of
moorland. However, Tregonning Hill is one of the highest hills in
the area and offers excellent views both inland and down to the sea.
The walk covers thousands of years of history, from the Iron Age remains on Tregonning Hill to Godolphin House, a little-known
stately home dating from the 15th century. Overall, this highly original route offers a taste of inland Cornwall about its business – from
working farms to country estates, with some breathtaking views
thrown in for good measure.

The route starts in the pretty hamlet of Germoe, which is dominated by the
church. This has been a consecrated site since the Dark Ages, when Christianity gained a foothold in the south-west due to the arrival of holy men and
women from Ireland. The new religion gathered strength, for many centuries
unchallenged in the area by the barbarian Saxons who were invading Britain
from the east. Germochus and his sister Breaca were two such holy people.
On landing at Hayle, they escaped the clutches of the local chieftain, Teudar, who was notoriously and lethally anti-Christian, and made their way to
Tregonning, where there was a large hill fort.

No remains of the earliest church survive today – it was probably made of

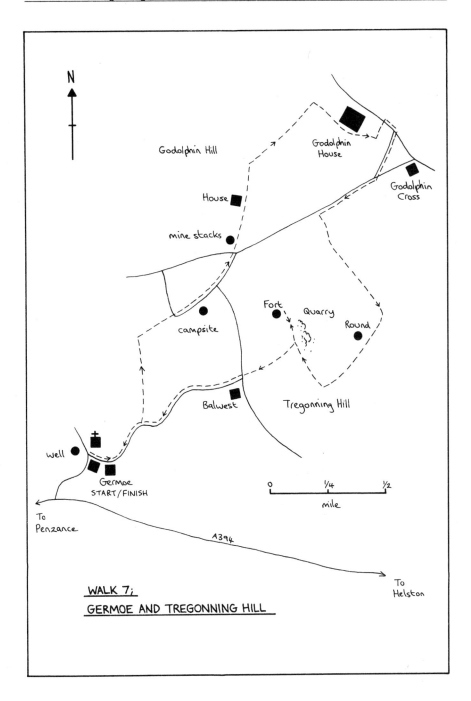

N

Godolphin Hill

Godolphin House

Godolphin Cross

House

mine stacks

Fort

Quarry

Round

campsite

Balwest

Tregonning Hill

Well

Germoe
START/FINISH

To Penzance

A394

0   ¼   ½
mile

To Helston

WALK 7;
GERMOE AND TREGONNING HILL

wood initially. The oldest parts of the church seen today date from the 12th century. These include the southern walls of the nave, the chancel and the south transept. It was William fitz Robert who built the original Norman cruciform church, although in the 13th century it was given to the Abbey of Hayles in Gloucestershire, before then being given to the Crown during the Reformation.

Also of interest is Germoe's Chair, an early medieval arched edifice in the churchyard, probably used during Palm Sunday celebrations. St Germoe's Well lies in front of the church, a little to the west, on the left side of the road. Many churches in Cornwall were built on or near to the cells of early saints such as Germoe. These cells were located near to holy wells, which often have a Christian superstructure, but pre-Christian powers. Leland, the Tudor antiquary, records the well at Germoe in 1538. However, the well seen today dates from 1978, when it was refurbished after its destruction in 1905 as the result of road building.

From the centre of the village go right, following the lane roughly northeast past a footpath sign on the left (this returns to the church). Pass the house on the right marked Trethewey. Go past two fields and a track leading up to a gate before reaching a stile on the left. Follow the stiles across five fields, as marked on the map. This is a quite steep climb, but remember to turn around as there are some good views down towards the coast.

The final field leads to a track. Follow this around until it emerges on a small lane. Turn right, and at the next junction continue straight on, keeping the caravan site on the right. Go past the next road on the right. At the next junction take the footpath marked on the left, past the mine stacks. At the cottage, turn to the right, following the path around its perimeter until it comes to a waymarked wooden stile, Once over this, cross the field to the stone stile in the opposite wall. The path goes immediately left and over another stile on to the bottom of Godolphin Warren.

Follow the wall on the right as closely as possible through the maze of small paths, not forgetting to look up – there are wonderful views across the sweep of the countryside inland. As the path nears a wall directly in front, there is a steel gate down to the right, by the trees. Go through this and continue down the wide path into some woodland. After a relatively short distance, this goes right through an entrance in a wall, just before the back of Godolphin House, which can be seen directly ahead.

Godolphin House was once home to the earls of Godolphin who were, like the

Vyvyans of Trelowarren on the other side of Helston, prominent Royalists, with Sir Francis Godolphin fighting for Charles I in 1642 and his younger brother being killed in similar duties a year later. The house itself has important 17th-century additions, with some intriguing Tuscan columns. It is open to the public on certain days from May to September. If you wish to visit the house on one of the open days, go left, then right at the edge of the wood. Walk down to a lane then turn right for the entrance to the house.

From the back of the house, the path goes right, along the wall which surrounds it. Cross three fields, cutting diagonally left across the third to cross a stream. Make a sharp left along the back of some houses and on to the road. Turn right, walking past the garage, before taking the first road on the right, walking through the village of Godolphin. Once out of the village, take the second track on the left. Just past the house on the left is a wooden stile and footpath marker.

A hedge has been removed, so the pattern of the fields does not fit the map. However, aim for the entrance to the field which is diagonally on the left of the stile. Once through the gateway, turn right and follow the path up to Tregonning Farm, which can be seen across a few fields. Go through the farmyard (the dog is friendly), emerging at a T-junction with a small lane. This is the start of the climb up Tregonning Hill. Turn right. As the route climbs, it begins to narrow, degenerating into a path which can be a little overgrown in the summer and muddy in the winter. Once on the hill, the path forks. Take the path on the right, but don't worry – the side of the hill is a warren of small paths and they all lead to the summit.

Once out of cultivated land, a round can be seen on the right. It may be overgrown in the summer, but has a diameter of about 80 metres and is surrounded by a ditch over 1 metre in depth in places.

Once at the top of the hill, turn right – the trig. point is at the northern end of the plateau.

There are excellent views from all points. The hill itself has had quite an impact on the history of the area. It has been settled since at least the Iron Age, when Castle Pencaire Fort was built, or possibly even earlier. Parts of the fort remain and the war memorial next to the trig. point stands on top of one of the two stone ramparts. Originally, it would have been over 100 metres in length and the remains of about twenty round houses within its walls are still distinguishable. The hill has two further rounds, one already seen to the south-east and one to the north-east of the fort. The remains of an ancient field system can also be seen on this slope. Germoe's sister, Breaca, chose to settle here, whilst her brother continued down to the valley below.

Much of this can be difficult to distinguish, however, because of more recent uses of the hill. Just over two hundred and fifty years ago, Tregonning was the site of the birth of a whole new industry for the South West – china clay. It was discovered on the slopes of the hill by William Cookworthy in 1746, and is one industry in the region that is still alive and kicking. Although now centred mainly on the St Austell area, there are still mines in Penwith, most notably Castle-An-Dinas, just north-east of Penzance and also the site of a magnificent Iron Age fort. Originally used to make porcelain, china clay is used today in the production of paper and chemicals, as well as other industries.

Leave the hill on the opposite side, taking the path on the right as the path back down from the memorial comes to a junction. The path ahead at this point leads to the other end of the hill. The path down the hill is wide and cobbled, descending to the hamlet of Balwest. Go through the village and turn right at the fork after the chapel, then follow the lane back into Germoe.

# 8. Loe Pool and Porthleven

**Route:**     Porthleven – Loe Pool – Penrose Estate – Settlement – Porthleven.

**Distance:**     5¼ miles

**Time:**     2½ hours

**Terrain:**     Easy. Mostly coastal, with some farmland.

**Refreshments:** Porthleven

**Access:**     By car – Porthleven is on the B3304, off the A394 from Helston to Penzance. By bus – 10 minutes from Helston or 30 minutes from Penzance on Western National, see end of chapter for details.

**Maps:**     Ordnance Survey Explorer 8 The Lizard, Ordnance Survey Landranger 203 Land's End.

This is a walk of surprises. The sheltered harbour of Porthleven gives no hint of the dramatic coastline just around the corner. Similarly, the coastal path does not prepare the unsuspecting walker for the wide, calm expanse of Cornwall's largest lake, with its many legends and a reputation for the taking of life. In turn, the leafy valley of the Penrose estate is in direct contrast both to the vast seascape on its doorstep and to the busy fishing village where the walk begins.

The walk starts at the harbour head, by the bus stop, looking down across the three sections of the Victorian harbour.

The inner section can be sealed off from the huge seas sometimes whipped up by south-westerly gales, protecting the boats moored there in almost calm water. Although much of the harbour area was built in the Victorian period or later, Porthleven's history goes back much further than that.

The name of the village means 'port of St Elvan', who was one of the many Celtic saints to have spread Christianity throughout the West Country in the Dark Ages. The village grew out of farming, mining and fishing, but the latter has declined dramatically all over the region. In 1897 there were 128 pilchard trawlers here, now there are none. Although a few working boats still remain, the once abundant pilchard is but a memory. Smuggling was once big business here, too. In the 17th and 18th centuries, The Ship was a well-known smuggling inn, and Methleigh Manor has several tunnels leading down to the west side of the harbour and coast, now sadly silted up.

The walk goes down the east side of the harbour and past the clock tower which dominates the skyline. Follow the road around to the left and be ready for the drama of cliffs and coves which continues right around to the Lizard itself. Go on up the road, always going right at forks in the road and staying as close to the beach as possible. After about ten minutes, the cottages of the village are left behind and the road sweeps down past a hotel on the right and into a small National Trust car park. Climb the steps which zigzag up the cliff at the far end, then follow the main path along the top, looking down on the beach.

The path emerges at Loe Pool, an unusual freshwater lake, divided from the sea by a single bar of sand. Tennyson called this lake a 'great water'. It was created in the 13th century by a huge storm and has remained due to the silt brought down the River Cober, whose waters now feed the lake. Before this, Helston was a port, with the ships carrying the locally streamed tin from the mines. After this no longer became possible, nearby Gweek, at the head of the Helford river, was used as the main port. Mining was the backbone of the local economy for more than 100 years, making Helston one of only a handful of coinage towns in Cornwall. At the peak of production, more than 30 mines were fully operational, and it was not until the early part of this century that the last one closed.

The Bar has taken many lives over the centuries as ships have tried to run for what they believed to be safety in a storm, or have even deliberately driven onto the beach in a last, desperate attempt to avoid the treacherous rocks. It was such a disaster in 1807, when the Anson ran aground, with the loss of hundreds of lives, which motivated Henry Trengrouse to try to help rescue attempts. He invented the rocket life-saver in 1816, which saved many lives, yet he died obscure and penniless.

The path swings left up the bank of the pool. Turn left through the gate of Bar Lodge immediately before the descent onto the beach. Go past the National Trust information point and follow the wide track through the woodland.

Over to the right, in the springtime, the shingle bank of the Bar is bright with the yellow horned poppy, distinguished by its deeply lobed petals and extremely long seed capsule. There are also some good views across the lake through the trees. This is a popular place for ornithologists, with many spe-

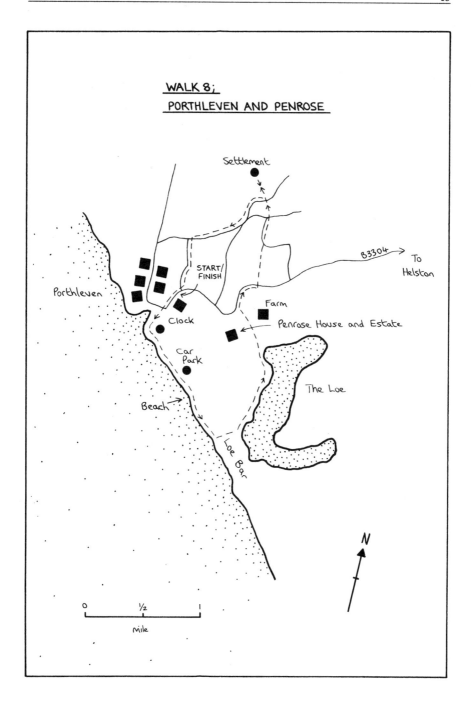

WALK 8;
PORTHLEVEN AND PENROSE

cies of birds in evidence, including rare migrants such as ospreys, as well as the more common kingfishers, cormorants and mute swans.

Tennyson used Loe Pool in his work *Morte D'Arthur*, suggesting that it was at Porthleven Sands that Arthur fought Mordred and that Excalibur was thrown into Loe Pool – across which Arthur was taken to Avalon by the Ladies of the Lake. This seems a less fanciful tale if one walks around the lake in a misty twilight when it certainly has an air of mystery. This is emphasised by the large population of bats of various species which can be seen hunting at twilight. Their favourite foods are insects and moths such as the yellow underwing.

In previous centuries, the Pool was of great botanical importance, but many of the species recorded are now extinct or have not been seen for many years. At the water's edge are plants such as water mint and meadowsweet. Visitors may also be astonished by the unusual colour of the water in the summer. This is due to algae which, helped by pollution, can grow very rapidly, and which in this case is very poisonous to all creatures.

The path emerges on open parkland in front of Penrose House (not open to the public). Cross the 19th-century bridge and turn left at the T-junction, following the sign for Porthleven.

From here you have the best views of the house, which was built in the 17th century, with the earliest record of a house here dating from 1281. The house was given to the Trust in 1974, making it only the third owner in 700 years.

At the fork in the path on the far side of the house, continue straight on, ignoring the route up to the left into the woods. The track ends on the B3304, at the bottom of Penrose Hill. Turn right up the road and walk for a few hundred metres (taking care on the bends), then go left through the metal gate into a field opposite the driveway to Lower Lanner Farm. Stay close to the hedge on the right, as the path goes through three fields before becoming a track which goes through Venton Vedna (the dog here can be a little unfriendly). This joins a small lane. Continue straight on, until a T-junction. Directly ahead there is a stone stile in the hedge. Cross this and go through two fields, with the hedge first on the right, then the left. This again emerges on a small country lane, but directly opposite is the footpath sign for Antron.

This place goes by the old name for Porthleven – St Elvan. It is little more than a house and an ancient settlement. There is little record of this saint, the only known written life of St Elvan disappeared from the church at Breage sometime after 1538. He was very probably Elwyn, who came over from Ireland with a band of other missionaries including Breaca, who later gave her name to Breage and Gwinear. Elwyn lost his head to the local king, Teudar.

The path to the settlement runs between two banks before opening out into a circular field bounded by a high hedge.

This is a round, probably dating from the Iron Age or slightly later. The Iron Age was a time of warrior aristocracies and rounds were smaller versions of hilltop forts, built to defend a single homestead rather than an entire community. This one measures 62 metres in diameter, with the remaining perimeter walls standing up to 2.5 metres in height.

Do not continue on the footpath to Antron, but retrace the path to the lane and turn right and then right again at the next crossroads. This is Torlevean Road, meaning 'farm of St Elvan'. Follow this, taking the road on the left at the next fork, which goes down and back to the harbour head.

Here the opportunity to follow in the footsteps of Porthleven's smugglers presents itself – have a drink in the old pub (strictly contraband-free).

*Porthleven*

# 9. Kynance Cove and the Lizard

**Route:**        Kynance Cove – Lizard Village – Signalling Station –
                  Lizard Point – Caerthillian Nature Reserve – Kynance
                  Cove.

**Distance:**     4½ miles

**Time:**         2¼ hours

**Terrain:**      Easy. Mostly coastal.

**Refreshments:** Lizard Village and Lizard Point

**Access:**       Follow the sign for Kynance and turn right off the A3083,
                  down a small lane just before Lizard Village. By bus,
                  change at Helston. See end of chapter for details.

**Maps:**         Ordnance Survey Explorer 8 The Lizard, Ordnance
                  Survey Landranger 203.

Opinion is divided as to the origin of the name 'Lizard'. Some think it is due to the shape of the peninsula as seen from sea, or perhaps it comes from 'Lis-arth' meaning 'high court' or 'fortress'. It did once have another name, one which still features in street and parish, that of 'meneage', meaning 'monk's land'. The origins of this are equally as hazy, but one thing is certain, the Lizard Peninsula has an atmosphere all of its own. From the secret wooded valleys of the Helford river, to the windswept and lonely expanse of the Goonhilly Downs, this is home to rare plants, beautiful coves and a dramatic history. A lifetime is not long enough to explore it, but an afternoon is certainly long enough to be captivated by it.

The walk starts from the National Trust car park above Kynance Cove.

This is the most colourful and unusual cove in Cornwall, if not in Britain. The golden beach is not large, but it faces south and is backed by high cliffs. The very name is from 'Kenans' meaning 'enclosed valley'. In the mouth of the cove are several islands, the most notable of which is the conical Asparagus Island (so named because wild asparagus does grow on it). The sea is always turquoise, due to the sandy bottom, and the serpentine rock shimmers green, pink, blue and purple in the sunshine.

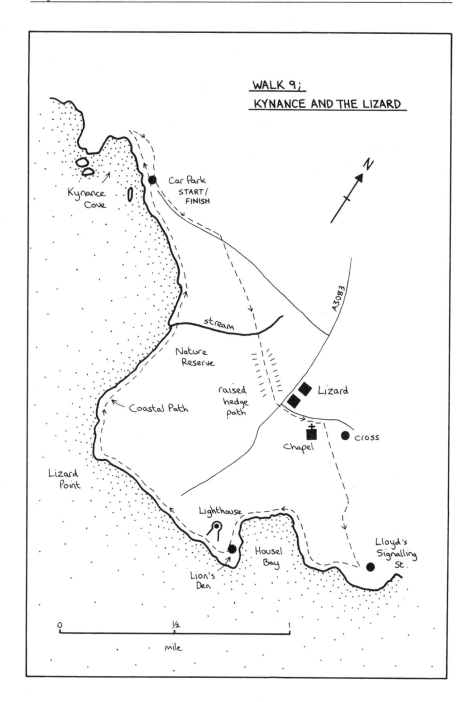

WALK 9;
KYNANCE AND THE LIZARD

N

Kynance
Cove

Car Park
START/
FINISH

A3083

stream

Nature
Reserve

Coastal Path

raised
hedge
path

Lizard

Chapel

Cross

Lizard
Point

Lighthouse

Lion's
Den

Housel
Bay

Lloyd's
Signalling
St.

0                    ½                    1

mile

It is the serpentine rock which is largely responsible for much which is unique about the peninsula. It is one of the reasons why the area supports many rare plants and animals. It is also an excellent raw material for carving and the Lizard village produces many different and beautiful products, including jewellery. It is not surprising, therefore, that this cove has been popular with visitors since the 19th century. Prince Albert brought his children here in 1846. Lord Tennyson also visited that year, and again in 1860. However, the cove is much less commercialised now than during this period. Since it was acquired by the Trust in 1986, the cove has been managed for conservation and several buildings demolished.

**From the car park, walk back up the lane towards the main road.**

This short section offers a better look at the moorland and closer inspection reveals a much richer environment than at first suspected. Many rare plants, such as orchids, grow here and the walk later includes a nature reserve.

**A few hundred metres past the white house on the right is a footpath sign pointing towards the Lizard village. Climb over the stile into the field and follow the line of stiles (large, wooden and difficult to miss) across several more fields. The last contains small trees and scrub, and has a stream running through it. Cross this and continue on a path which runs along the top of a turf-topped 'stone hedge'.**

Attempts to cultivate the downs have been made since the Middle Ages and many similar walls which support paths were built after the Enclosure Acts of the 19th century. These unusual paths have been recorded since the last century, and have probably been a feature of the area for much longer than that. The cultivation of the downs is also still a feature, made easier by modern farming techniques. In the last 25 years, a quarter of the heathland has been lost to agriculture.

**The elevated path ends at a small lane. Turn left by the crossroads sign and walk into the centre of the village,. Keep straight, crossing the main road, and following a road lined with houses past the chapel and school. The second footpath sign on the right points down a wide, potholed track.**

Before turning down this, however, look a few metres up the road to the cross at the junction. Straight ahead there is a wheel-headed cross with a Latin cross in relief. It is probably a wayside cross, marking the route to church, or possibly a boundary cross, showing the limits of glebe land.

*Kynance Cove*

Walk down the track, known as Lloyd's Road, heading towards the large, white, castellated building on the coast.

This was the signalling station used to send and receive messages from passing ships before the invention of the electric telegraph. This was achieved by the use of a system of flags.

Just before the driveway up to the building, there is a faded, wooden sign-post pointing to the right, down to the coastal path. This is now followed all the way back to Kynance.

The first bay the path comes to is Housel, the location of Britain's most southerly hotel, which has had some famous guests in its time, including C.S. Lewis and King George V. The location is certainly magnificent, with Atlantic breakers crashing on the tall cliffs in even the calmest weather.

The path becomes a short climb after this, but just before it rounds the corner and swings up to the lighthouse, there is a curious geological phenomenon.

On the left of the path there is a huge crater in the ground known as Lion's Den. It is two hundred feet (65 metres) in depth, but unfenced and dangerous for unattended children and animals. This immense hole in the ground was created one night in 1847 when a sea cave collapsed. The earth and rock which subsided has since been washed out to sea so only the crater remains, waiting to catch an unwary walker in the fog or darkness!

On the right, a few metres after this is the lighthouse. A light was first put here, amid much controversy, in 1619 by Sir John Killigrew. Shipowners accused him of placing the light at this point to ensure any ships wrecked were lost further up the coast on his land, whilst local inhabitants opposed the light because it would rob them of 'God's Grace', the bounty from (innocently) wrecked ships. It wasn't until 1752 that a light was firmly established here and today it is one of the most modern in the country, leading the move towards unmanned, computer-controlled lights. The lighthouse is not open to visitors.

A short distance further and the route emerges at the most southerly point in Britain. It was from here that the Armada was first sighted in 1588 and a chain of fires lit across the county to send warning of the invasion. There is a road down to here, and in summertime a small café does brisk business.

**The path continues a few metres up the road, following another faded coastal path sign on the left. This goes past the old lifeboat house and down into Pistil Meadow.**

This place is heavy with history, although not, as one might assume, with pistol duels at dawn. The name may have come from the wreck of the *Royal Anne* in 1720, when crates of guns were washed ashore, although it is much more likely to have an older origin, dating back to pre-Roman times, as the Celtic word 'pystil' means 'waterfall'. There is one here, but it can best be seen from the sea. It was also in this meadow during the 1700s that the dead from a wrecked ship were buried in a mass grave and unsurprisingly, several tales of its haunting are still told.

**The path continues around this dramatic and tragic coastline.**

The names of ships wrecked here over the centuries would cover many pages and it is easy to see why – the spiky, black bones of reefs and half-submerged islands turn the sea into churning white foam, even on a fairly calm day. On this eastern side of the peninsula, walkers can look west across Mount's Bay to the Land's End peninsula, a place as wild and varied as the Lizard.

At Caerthillian Cove, the path crosses part of a national nature reserve, managed by English Nature.

The Lizard is important for animals, insects and plants for several reasons. The almost unique rock is one reason, and the climate and relative lack of agricultural disturbance help create a very special habitat. Many rare plants flourish here, including Cornish Heath, a pinkish-white heather which flowers in late summer, rare clover and other grassland species. The site is also important to creatures. Several rare types of spider live here, as does a species of moth only recently discovered. Take care when walking and keep to the path as many of the plants cannot survive being stepped on.

Between Caerthillian and Kynance, the path forks. Left is marked for the beach and right as the coastal path. Take the latter, following it along the top of the headland, and enjoying some spectacular views as it approaches the cove. The walker can then choose to either turn right into the car park or to continue down into the cove for one last look!

# 10. Helford and Frenchman's Creek

**Route:**        Helford – Frenchman's Creek – Penarvon Cove – Helford.

**Distance:**    2½ miles

**Time:**          1½ hours

**Terrain:**      Easy. The route combines woodland and farmland
                   walking. The latter can be very muddy after any rain,
                   especially through the farmyard at Kestle, so suitable
                   footwear is essential.

**Refreshments:** Helford

**Access:**      Helford is situated on the east side of the Lizard
                  Peninsula, south of the Helford river. The nearest main
                  road is the B3293, which joins with the A3083 to Helston.
                  Follow the signposts from the B road to Helford. Parking is
                  on the right, above the village.

**Maps:**        Ordnance Survey Explorer 8 The Lizard and Ordnance
                  Survey Landranger 204.

---

This walk encompasses what is, for many people, the essence of Cornwall. The banks of the Helford River hang verdant and tranquil over the slow-moving water, with only the occasional heron or sailboat to mar the peace. Numerous creeks reach up into wooded valleys, often accessible only by water. Frenchman's Creek is the most famous of these, yet despite this it still retains a magical, almost eerie beauty.

The walk starts from the car park by the river, before the road enters the village.

> This open area has wonderful views across the river to the hamlet of Helford Passage on the opposite side. It is difficult to believe that the flat, windswept moorland of Goonhilly Downs is only a few miles away from this impossibly picturesque landscape.

From the car park, turn right down the road into Helford.

> This hamlet is little more than the head of a creek lined with old cottages, many of which are thatched, as is the perfectly situated pub. It was here

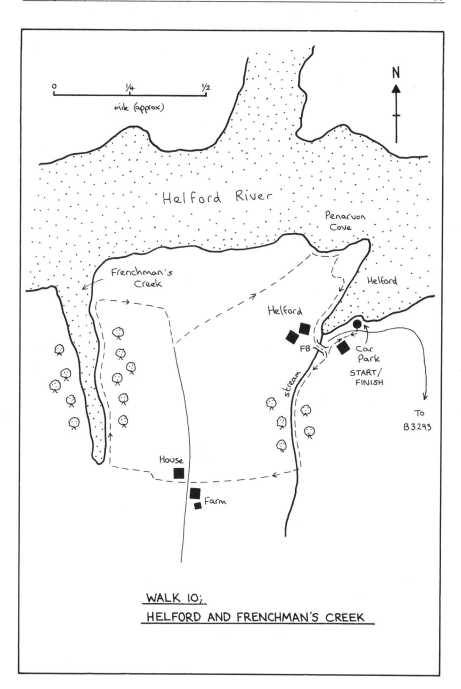

WALK 10;
HELFORD AND FRENCHMAN'S CREEK

that Captain Bligh of the *Bounty* was mistaken for a French spy and arrested. It is not difficult to see how such an accident could occur. This area was one of the most notorious in a region which was infamous for its smuggling activities. The countless creeks covered in dense woodland provided the perfect cover for the so-called 'free traders' of the 18th and 19th centuries, who smuggled salt, brandy, tobacco and other taxable contraband in, whilst smuggling wool, subject to excise duty, out. It was this colourful history that Daphne Du Maurier drew on when she wrote *Frenchman's Creek*.

Do not cross the footbridge but continue along the lane, following the footpath sign for Manaccan up a concrete track. Turn right at the fork on the path which passes behind a white, thatched cottage.

This path leads into an area of woodland which is pretty at any time of the year.

At the next fork, cross the stream and take the path up on the right for a short distance before crossing a stone stile into a field. Keep the hedge on the right and climb up to the gate into the farmyard. Cross the yard, walking to the left of the farmhouse and passing through a gate with a yellow arrow on it. Cross the road, following the footpath sign down the field, keeping to the right, until the first gate on the right, at the end of the buildings. Go through this, then turn immediately left down a track through some more woodland. At the next fork, go right again, following the sign indicating a permissive path to Frenchman's Creek.

The still, perfect beauty of this forgotten spot captured the imagination of writer Daphne Du Maurier when she spent her honeymoon sailing up the Helford river in 1932. She subsequently made the creek famous in her novel of the same name, based on the rich smuggling history of the area. Her book evokes the atmosphere of the place exactly, woven into a tale of passion and high adventure.

The path crosses two footbridges, then forks. Take the path on the right up the steps.

At the top of these, the walker is rewarded with fabulous views up the river towards Gweek and the entrance to Frenchman's Creek, or simply the 'pill' as it's locally known, this unusual word meaning 'pool' or 'creek' in Cornish. There is a wooden bench here and a few moments of silent contemplation may be rewarded with a sighting of some of the many sea and river birds attracted to the estuary and its mud flats, including that elusive dash of brilliance, the kingfisher.

Continuing on, the path comes to a kissing gate. Turn right up the lane after this, then right again at a track marked as the route to Helford via Penarvon Cove. At the cattle grid, turn left, down a lane signposted to Pengwedhen. The route has now re-entered woodland and this quiet lane could be a thousand miles away from the popularity of Helford in high summer.

Continue straight at the fork to reach, a short time later, the tiny beach at Penarvon, with its scattering of cottages. Turn right and cross the top edge of the beach, turning right into the woods, then immediately left

along a path which climbs up through the woods to join a wall on the right. Follow the path as it goes through some houses and a small, metal gate. At the T-junction, turn left past the white house, then right, passing the pub in Helford. To reach the passenger ferry to Helford Passage, turn left and follow the small tarmac path along the bank of the creek until it joins with the river. To return to the start of the walk, continue through the village, crossing the footbridge and turning left up to the car park.

*Helford Creek*

# 11. Mawnan Smith and the Gardens of the Helford River

**Route:**          Mawnan Smith – Carwinnion Gardens – Porth Saxon –
                    Durgan – Trebah and Polgwiddon Cove – Helford
                    Passage – Penpol – Mawnan Smith.

**Distance:**       4 miles

**Time:**           2 hours

**Terrain:**        Easy. Mostly by the river, with some farmland.

**Refreshments:** Mawnan Smith, Helford Passage.

**Access:**         By car, this walk is easily accessed from either Falmouth
                    (signposted) or from the A394 to the north-west. By bus,
                    the easiest approach is from Falmouth. Check details at
                    the end of the chapter.

**Maps:**           Ordnance Survey Explorer 8 The Lizard, Ordnance
                    Survey Landranger 204.

This walk is fascinating because of the contrast between the cultivated, sub-tropical gardens and the stretches of native woodland
and wildflowers which line the river. Ideal for both natural historians and those taking a Sunday afternoon stroll, this walk includes
some of the prettiest and most gentle countryside in the west of the
county. The route runs mostly alongside the mouth of the famous
and beautiful Helford river. This is a wonderfully lush part of the
peninsula, seemingly a million miles from the windswept and
lonely Goonhilly Downs, just south-west of here. The climate is so
mild that sub-tropical plants flourish and this walk includes the opportunity to explore three of the best gardens in the area.

The walk starts from the centre of the village, at the thatched pub called
The Red Lion. From here, go south down the road to the left, past the
shops. Just before the village ends, there is the second of two footpath
signs on the right. This points down a track, just prior to the entrance for
Carwinion Gardens. This becomes a path and swings to the left before

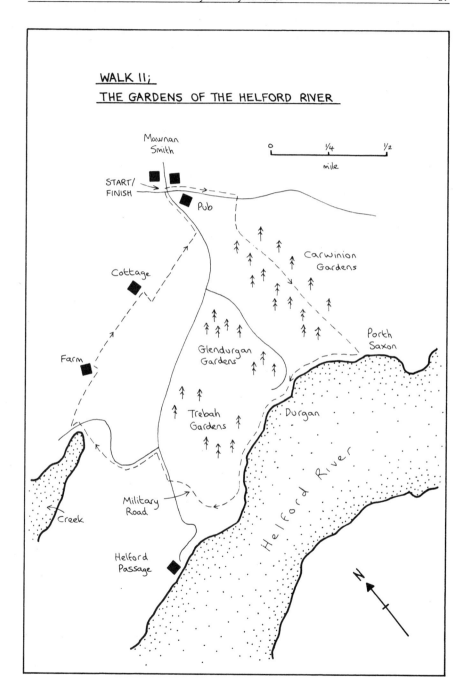

WALK II;
THE GARDENS OF THE HELFORD RIVER

crossing a stile marked as the path to Porth Sawson. Follow the main path along the valley floor, going through several gates.

This tranquil woodland, which is so pretty at any time of the year, is but a foretaste of what is to come.

The path eventually emerges at a small beach, with good views across the mouth of this famous river to Dennis Head.

It was on the rocks here in 1891 that the region witnessed one of the worst shipwrecks in its history. That year saw the worst weather in over 200 years and the four-masted *Bay of Panama* was caught by dense blizzards and huge seas. Many of the crew were washed overboard, but some clung to the rigging as the square-rigger was dashed on the rocks. The story did not end there as the few men who were rescued were later caught in another blizzard whilst on their way to Falmouth, being forced to walk the last six miles in deep snow or be frozen to death.

From the cove, turn right, following the coastal path up towards the mouth of the river. The path forks at several points, but stick to the river's edge, keeping Bosloe House on the right. The path emerges just above the tiny hamlet of Durgan.

This is partly owned by the National Trust, and is the first point of shelter for vessels coming up the river where landing is possible at all states of the tide. The hamlet has access to Glendurgan Gardens ( if visited, please pay at the entrance at the top of the valley), through a wooden gate at the back of the village. The gardens were planted in the early 1800s by the Fox family, who are still the principal shipping agents in Falmouth. Many of the gardens in this area owe a debt to the family, who had various species of plants brought from around the world to the warm, damp climate of the Helford. Such plants include tulip trees, Mexican cypresses, Monterey pines and deodar cedars from the Himalayas. The gardens also have a maze, planted in laurel in 1833, and are open from March to October.

Even the woodland outside the perimeter of the gardens shows evidence of planting, with maple and sweet chestnut mixed in with oak, sycamore and ash. The path here is overhung by the brilliant yellows of gorse and honeysuckle, and the ever present sea campion.

From Durgan, re-join the coastal path by walking past Post Box Cottage. After about fifty metres, take a sharp left which doubles back above the village and then swings right to continue along the river's edge. A short distance later, the next little cove offers the chance to visit Trebah Gardens.

These gardens, like Glendurgan, have many exotic sub-tropical plants such as bamboo thriving in the shelter of the valley. Again, pay at the entrance if visiting the gardens.

The path goes behind the small beach, with the gardens on the right, along a concrete path. At the end of the cove, this slopes uphill and goes through a gate, next to a Countryside Commission sign showing the area conserved and open to the public. From here, there is a choice. A few metres further along the concrete, the coastal path branches to the left (look for the marker) and then into Helford Passage, where there is a 16th-century pub, mostly rebuilt in the 1930s, which is a Mecca for yachting types. Alternatively, continue along the concrete track, which slopes uphill, cutting off the corner of Helford Passage itself.

This area was used to train and accommodate US troops prior to the D-Day landings, and tank tracks can still be seen in the concrete. It was from the unlikely Trebah beach that sections of the Mulberry Harbour were shipped, for use off the beaches of France.

The area of grassy scrub is perfect for both birds such as skylarks and earthbound creatures, such as weasels and rabbits. Flowers love this habitat too, with wild rose and bulbous buttercup giving way to the bright yellow and red berries of bryony in the autumn. Many different varieties of grass flower also, including all three types of trefoil, a member of the clover family. From here there is a good view of the river winding its way inland, with Helford village a short ferry ride away across Monk's Passage.

The concrete ends 100 metres or so from the road which goes down to Helford Passage, but the path continues across the grass and through a gate to the road. Turn right and walk up the road.

The granite walls here are home to another, entirely different set of wild plants. Ferns in particular find purchase in the cracks. Watch for the oval lobes on either side of the stem of maidenhair spleenwort and, of course, the common hart's tongue. Other hedgerow plants in the area include wild strawberry and red campion.

On reaching the junction, turn left. After a short distance there is a footpath sign pointing across a field just inside a driveway. Go down here and through a small gap at the bottom on to a small lane. Cross the small bridge at the head of the creek.

This widens out into Porth Navas Creek, with the village of the same name located on the opposite bank, a little closer to the river. There have been oyster beds harvested here since Roman times. The present day farm is owned by the Duchy, which grows oysters for consumption all over the country.

On the far side of the bridge there is a footpath sign pointing up a track to Lower Penpol Farm. Follow this up into the farmyard, then swing right through the metal gates (following a handmade sign) along a short, but exceptionally muddy (and not necessarily just mud!) track into the first of two fields. Keep to the left hedge and go through the gate by the cottage. Turn right in front of this, then follow the footpath sign over a stone stile. Follow the path through three more fields before crossing another stile and following the path between two fences and back to the road. Turn left and it will shortly bring you back to the crossroads by the pub.

# 12. Carn Brea

| | |
|---|---|
| **Route:** | Castle – Great Flat Lode Trail – Monument – Hut Circles. |
| **Distance:** | 1¼ miles |
| **Time:** | 1 hour |
| **Terrain:** | Moderate. Some steep climbs and descents. |
| **Refreshments:** | Restaurant at the castle. |
| **Access:** | From Carnkie, follow the lane marked 'castle' (deteriorates into a poor track) to unofficial parking between the summits. |
| **Maps:** | Ordnance Survey Explorer 104 Redruth and St Agnes, Ordnance Survey Landranger 203 Land's End. |

This may be a short walk, but virtually every step brings something new and of interest, not least the fabulous views from the summit. At 825ft (225 metres), the panorama extends from St Michael's Mount and the hills of West Penwith to the China Clay Mines at St Austell. It also gives an almost map-like view of the layout of this formerly industrial district and it is possible to discern the old mine workings in amongst the modern roads and light industrial units. Both ancient and modern history have left their mark on the Redruth district and nowhere more so than at Carn Brea, once at the heart of the richest centre of mining in Cornwall. Considering this, it is surprising how little remains, yet there is quite enough to catch the interest of the curious walker.

It may seem like cheating, parking on the saddle just below the summit, but rest assured, that steep flank of muddy hillside will be assailed (those who chose this walk on the basis of brevity – be warned!). The castle is over to the right. This rather endearing little building is probably best described as a 'hunting lodge' as this was its primary role in life. Built in the 15th century, when these slopes were thickly forested, it has had several major restorations in the intervening centuries and now leads a more demure existence as a restaurant.

Follow the track up to the castle entrance, then take the narrow path downhill, heading towards the church. This is very steep and can be muddy and slippery after rain. At the base of the hill there is a wide track. Turn left on to this and follow it around the base, passing a sign marked 'Great Flat Lode Trail', so named due to the Basset Mines to the south of Carnkie.

On the right of this path are the few remains of Carn Brea Mine, which was worked for copper from 1831 to 1881, when production switched to tin, before closing in 1921. Over 1000 people were employed on this mine alone, with well over 30 times that number working in associated industries in the area. The mines were supported by mineral tramways which transported the ores to Devoran on the south coast and Hayle and Portreath on the north coast.

It is easy to lose the route in a maze of pathways along the base of the hill. Follow the waymarkers with yellow arrows. There is one on the left, through a gap in a hedge at a fork in the path. Continue along this path to a second yellow marker, which points to a path which goes directly up the middle of the north side of Carn Brea, passing a quarry on the right. This would have produced materials for the mine workings.

The path keeps to the left of a hedge and ends at a crossroads in the pathways, just to the west of the monument. Turn left, passing through a gap in the remains of the ancient defences on the hilltop

From here it is easier to appreciate why the place was chosen as early as the Neolithic period for a settlement. The natural defences are outstanding. The steep sides of the hill are topped with another natural barrier — rocky outcrops, such as those by the castle. There are two different defence systems here. The outer ramparts are Iron Age in origin and enclose the two eastern summits, the castle and the monument, in approximately 16 hectares of land. Parts of the remaining defences stand to a height of over 3 metres.

However, there is a smaller, stone-walled enclosure around the castle. This probably dates to the Neolithic period and extensive excavation work was carried out here in the 1970s. It was discovered to be 6000 years old, and one of Britain's oldest known settlements. Several hundred flint arrowheads were found here, indicating a battle, or invasion. Possibly the most astonishing fact about this site is the length of its occupation. It is difficult to know if the fort was continuously occupied, but aside from the Neolithic remains, there are also Iron Age remains, including the clear outline of some round houses, and coins from the early Roman period were found here in 1749, with some Celtic coins from the south-east and Gaul.

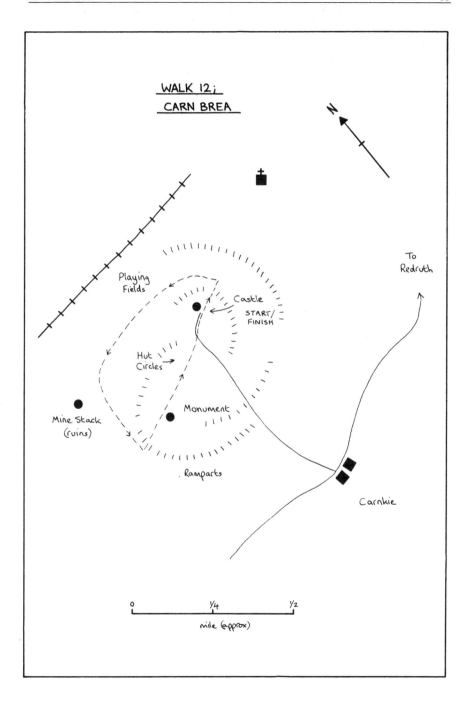

WALK 12;
CARN BREA

N

To
Redruth

Playing
Fields

Castle
START/
FINISH

Hut
Circles

Mine Stack
(ruins)

Monument

Ramparts

Carnkie

0          ¼          ½

mile (approx)

*Monument on Carn Brea*

The huge piles of stone, not unlike those found on parts of Bodmin Moor, have several legends attached to them. One version of the story suggests that the giant of Carn Brea fought with the giant on St Agnes Beacon, using rocks as missiles. Another version suggests that the battle was between the saints of Cornwall and Satan, using the rocks as weapons. It may be a relief to know that Satan lost, but be warned – he did not leave the entire county!

## Continue east, towards the monument.

This huge pillar can be seen for miles and was built in 1836, thanks to public subscription, in memory of Francis Basset, Lord of Dunstanville and a member of the Tehidy family, who made their fortune in mining. Francis was something of a philanthropist, concerning himself with the plight of the poor in area. To this end, he founded the Royal Infirmary in Truro, built a harbour at storm-wrecked Portreath and was a supporter of Trevithick and his work with high pressure steam engines.

## From the monument back to the start, there are some excellent remains of round houses.

These probably date from the Iron Age. Bracken may obscure them in summer, but careful exploration will be rewarded as several lie just to the side of the path. Also located between the monument and the castle is a smugglers' cave. Noted several times by different writers in the past century, it is said to be just to the west of the 'gate' in the northern rampart. During the time of intense smuggling activity in the 18th century, many tunnels for-

*Castle on Carn Brea*

merly used in mining were adapted for the secret storage and transport of contraband. This cave on Carn Brea is said to connect with a continuous network from Godrevy near Hayle, to Stithians. In the 1980s, however, it was found to be blocked, with only the entrance visible. This writer failed to find it, but anyone with a strong interest is encouraged to make a search through the gorse and bracken – you may make a discovery!

# Useful Information

**Transport in the Lizard Area:** Helston, Falmouth and Redruth are the main towns in this area. Redruth has a main line train station. For all rail enquires, call 0345 484950. All bus services around the Lizard Peninsula (which can be infrequent, with the exceptions of routes to Porthleven and Germoe) start from Coinagehall Street in Helston. Truronian buses to all points on Walk 11 leave from near the TIC in Falmouth (T#4). For local timetable information for Western National Services, call 01209 719988; for Truronian services, call 01872 273453.

**Other Information:** English Nature, The Lizard National Nature Reserve 01326 240808; Glendurgan Gardens (National Trust), open March-November (Walk 11) 01326 250906; Trebah Gardens, open all year (Walk 11) 01326 250448; Carwinnion Gardens, Mawnan Smith, open all year 01326 250258; Godolphin House, open various days May-September (Walk 7) 01736 762409.

English Heritage: http://www.cornwallonline.co.uk/english-heritage

Tourist Information Centres: Falmouth, 28 Killigrew St. 01326 312300; Helston and Lizard, 79 Meneage St. 01326 565431.

Youth Hostels: Pendennis Castle, Falmouth 01326 311435; Parc Behan, School Hill, Coverack 01326 280687.

# The
# North Coast

*Willapark Cliff Castle and lookout: see walk 17*

# 13. St Agnes and Chapel Porth

| | |
|---|---|
| **Route:** | St Agnes Beacon – St Agnes Head – Wheal Coates Mine – Chapel Porth – St Agnes Chapel (remains). |
| **Distance:** | 3½ miles |
| **Time:** | 2 hours |
| **Terrain:** | Easy to moderate. Mostly coastal, with one undemanding climb up to the Beacon. |
| **Refreshments:** | None on route. |
| **Access:** | The walk starts in the National Trust car park on Beacon Drive, on the western side of the Beacon. St Agnes itself is on the B3277, reached via the A30, north of Redruth. If using public transport, St Agnes can be reached from either Redruth or Truro. See end of chapter for details. |
| **Maps:** | Ordnance Survey Explorer 104 Redruth and St Agnes and Ordnance Survey Landranger 203 Land's End. |

The small town of St Agnes has a history as colourful as the landscape is stunning. It has been home to artists and philanthropists, as well as tin and copper mines. It inspired Winston Graham to use it as the model for the village of St Ann in the Poldark series, and its miners have always claimed 'Sten Sen Agnes an gwella sten yu Kernow' – 'St Agnes tin is the best tin in Cornwall'. This walk explores the history of the area, both ancient and modern, as well as including some of the most stunning scenery on the north coast.

From the car park, turn left up the road until the first lane on the right. This is a public right of way through Beacon Cottage Farm. Follow the lane around to the farmyard, then strike to the right and turn left through a field gate. Cross two fields, keeping the hedge on the left, until reaching the National Trust land at the southern base of the beacon. Continue along the base of the hill until a wide path strikes to the left, climbing the shoulder of the hill.

The summit's breathtaking views are the best in this part of Cornwall. The highest tors of Bodmin Moor can be seen to the east, whilst on a clear day, Carn Brea and St Ives can be seen in the far west. There are several cairns on

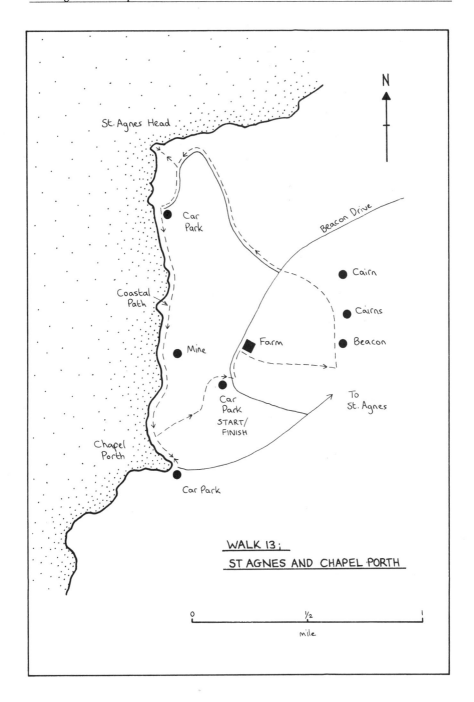

WALK 13;
ST AGNES AND CHAPEL PORTH

the summit of the beacon, probably dating from the Bronze Age. The most southerly is the easiest to discern, although they all lie close to the main path.

Continue along the plateau until a wide path swings down to the left, ending on Beacon Drive. Cross this and continue down the lane opposite, which leads to St Agnes Head. It soon leaves the fields behind for the gorse and heather of the headland. The lane passes a picnic area, then swings to the left, just short of the point itself, which is home to a coastguard station. When the lane ends in a small car park, continue along the coastal path until the remains of Wheal Coates Mine come into view.

The St Agnes area has been heavily mined over the centuries, producing tin, copper, iron, lead and silver. The remains of this industry can be seen everywhere, and there are even some open workings on the Beacon which may well be medieval. Wheal Coates Mine, with the Towanroath engine house perched on its photogenic yet dangerous ledge above the wild seas, has been partially restored by the National Trust. At the peak of its production, in the 1870s, a 36-inch pumping engine was installed, but the mine was never very productive and closed in 1889.

From the mine, continue along the coastal path, with its awe-inspiring views along the cruel northern cliffs.

The sea always appears an innocent pale turquoise here, due to the many sandy coves which tempt unwary swimmers into their treacherous depths. The pretty combe of Chapel Porth is one such cove. Although popular in the summertime, swimming can be extremely dangerous, with an undertow that caused problems even when the cove was a port for the mines. Although the main loading point was at Trevaunance Cove north of St Agnes Head, it, too, was ravaged by the huge seas which can be whipped up by winter storms in this area and, like Chapel Porth, was abandoned after the fourth harbour was swept away during the early part of this century.

Chapel Porth gets its name from a sacred well and the early Christian chapel built close by in the Dark Ages. The scant remains of this can be found (with a little luck) if the path is re-traced to the fork. At this point, take the path going inland and a few metres further on the outline of the chapel can be seen just to the right of the path.

Nothing now remains of the well, which was said to have curative and oracular properties, beliefs which originated during pagan times. Sacred places such as this were often later appropriated for the purposes of the new religion of Christianity. Such was the case here, with a small chapel built and dedicated to St Agnes. The saint was said to have been a Roman of high social standing who rejected the hand of a non-Christian. She was subsequently burnt, but the flames formed a circle around the stake, leaving her untouched. She was later beheaded – at the tender age of thirteen. After the waters of the well drained into the mine workings, the small chapel was demolished sometime at the end of the 18th century and its stones used to build a wall.

Continue along the path, going inland across the moorland. The path emerges into the car park and the start of the walk.

# 14. Perranporth and the Lost Lands

**Route:**          St Piran's Round – Penhale Dunes Nature Reserve – St
                    Piran's Church and Cross – St Piran's Oratory – Penhale
                    Sands.

**Distance:**       4½ miles

**Time:**           2¼ hours

**Terrain:**        Easy, although much of the walk is through sand dunes
                    and this can occasionally be more of a challenge.

**Refreshments:** None on route, although the town of Perranporth lies
                    close enough for a small detour, if necessary.

**Access:**         The walk starts from St Piran's Round, which lies off the
                    B3285 to Perranporth, accessed via the A3075, north of
                    Redruth. See end of chapter for public transport details.

**Maps:**           Ordnance Survey Explorer 104 Redruth and St Agnes,
                    Ordnance Survey Landranger 200.

As may be gathered from the route outline, there is something of a
theme to this walk. Not everything of interest on this walk is directly
related to Piran, however. There was a thriving community here
long before the arrival of the saint, but all traces of it are lost beneath
the ever shifting sand. At another point in the long and varied history of the town, Perranporth was a very productive mining area until the early part of this century. The arrival of a railway in 1906
introduced the town's three miles of beach to visitors. Now, the
branch line has gone, but the tourists have stayed and despite the
sprawl of caravan sites there is some good walking in the area, with
excellent views along the coast.

The walk starts at St Piran's Round, which is located on the north side of
the B3285, between Goonhavern and Perranporth. The turning is easily
missed, so watch for the pink B&B by the side of the road. The round is up
a short track opposite.

The 6th-century, Irish saint Piran certainly left his stamp in the county as
he passed through on his way to Brittany. He is credited with an impressive
knowledge of tin processing and is said to have passed on his secrets to the

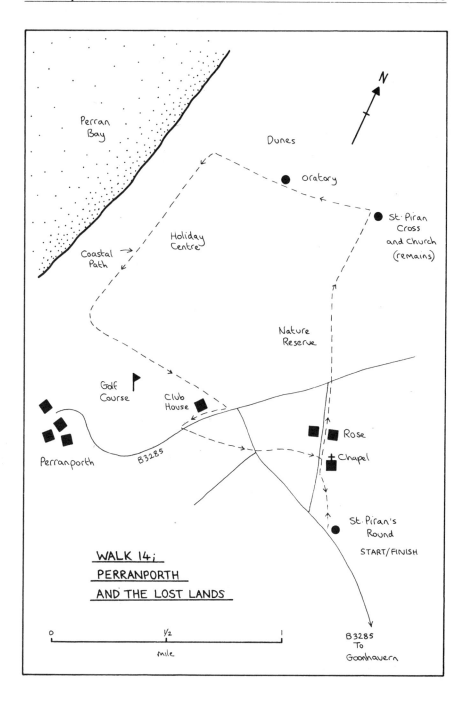

Perran Bay

Dunes

N

Oratory

St. Piran
Cross
and Church
(remains)

Holiday
Centre

Coastal
Path

Nature
Reserve

Golf
Course

Club
House

Rose

Perranporth

B3285

Chapel

St. Piran's
Round

START/FINISH

WALK 14;
PERRANPORTH
AND THE LOST LANDS

0          ½          1

mile

B3285
To
Goonhavern

miners of Cornwall, who have, in return, kept his memory alive so that today he is the patron saint of miners. His flag – a black cross on a white background – is the flag of Cornwall.

The round, which measures approximately 45 metres in diameter, was built during the late Iron Age, the earthen bank giving protection to the settlement within. Its useful life did not end there, however. Like several other rounds in Cornwall, most notably that of St Just in Penwith, it was used in the medieval era as a theatre, or 'plen-an-gwary'. These 'playing places' presented a cycle of works in Cornish called the Miracle Plays, which are still performed today. These represent the most significant body of work produced in Cornish literature, with the most important cycle, entitled Ordinalia, consisting of three plays covering *The Origin of the World* to *The Resurrection*.

From the south-east corner of the round enclosure, by the gate, take the track up to the left, past the white house. This leads shortly into the hamlet of Rose. Turn right and continue up the lane until a T-junction. Continue straight on here, following the footpath sign into the gorse. Almost immediately there is an information point on the right.

This is the entrance to Penhale Dunes, which have been designated a Site of Special Scientific Interest. Various types of rare fauna and flora can be found here, including the skylark, with its magical song once so common in the UK and now greatly threatened due to loss of habitat. There are also over two hundred different species of flowers, many of which are uncommon in the rest of the county. As one might expect in such an area, the dunes are a good place to butterfly watch, with many species in abundance, including some rarities.

After a short distance, the path leaves the gorse behind and emerges on the dunes, then splits. Follow the yellow acorn waymarkers for the coastal path. This swings to the right, going roughly north. However, pathways in sand dunes are notorious for fading away and re-emerging somewhere unexpected so, after walking a short distance, the round-headed cross (**not the traditional cross over to the left**) should come into view and this is our initial destination, should the path disappear beneath your feet!

This cross, with its unusual three holes, is almost unique in the county and dates from the late Dark Ages – around AD900. It stands only a few metres from the Norman church, built in 1150, which, like its Celtic predecessor

*St Piran's cross, Perranporth*

(encountered a little further on), was consumed by sand so that little more than ruins now remain.

From the cross, turn left, keeping the fence bordering the military area on the right. Another waymarker can be seen, showing the route along an easily definable sandy track to St Piran's Oratory.

This is said to be one of the oldest churches in the south-west. Nothing can be seen now, except a stone marking the site. The church still stands, however – below your feet. It was covered over for protection in 1980. This was done because the church had previously been buried beneath the sand for over a thousand years, reappearing during the last century.

St Piran was born in South-West Ireland and is said to have been a disciple of St Patrick's. On conversion to the new faith, he went to Rome for a time, but when he returned to Ireland so many came to his cell that he left, sailing – legend has it – for Cornwall on a millstone. His story is fairly common amongst early Christian saints, as it was only the far west – especially Ireland – that escaped invasion by the barbarian Saxons, allowing Christianity to flourish (albeit incorporating aspects of the older religion of paganism).

Continue along the wider path until it crests the final sand dune and a great expanse of sea and sky opens out.

Local legend states that Penhale Sands was once the site of a mighty city, called Langona, which had seven churches. However, the inhabitants invoked the wrath of God and the sand swept over the entire city, burying it forever. Like many legends, it probably has its origin in a kernel of truth. In this case, a settlement drowned by sand does not seem so unlikely when we know what happened to St Piran's Oratory.

Turn left and walk along the seaward edge of the sand dunes above the beach, keeping the caravan site on the left. After about a third of a mile, a concrete road from the caravan site goes down to the beach. At the far side of a small parking area there is another coastal path waymarker, indicating the true path for anyone wandering amongst the plethora of routes through the dunes.

This cliff top section ends as the cliff falls away on to the beach, and the walker can look down on the town which, with nearby St Agnes, provided the setting for Winston Graham's famous Poldark novels about life in the mining areas of 18th-century Cornwall.

Perranporth and the surrounding area was heavily mined during the 19th century, producing tin, copper, lead and even silver. Most important for Perranporth, however, was iron, with the Great Perran Iron Lode producing two hundred thousand tons in just over 30 years! It may come as a shock to some visitors to know that the entire area has been undermined, from the northern end of the beach to St Agnes.

At the end of the cliff, before the start of the beach, there is a path across the top of a golf course, which emerges on the B3285. This path is very difficult to follow and walkers may find themselves too far south and stumble across a lower footpath which started in the town itself. This path is waymarked with large, old wooden posts and passes behind the clubhouse before also reaching the B3285. The route home is directly across the road from here. The original, higher path across the golf course emerges a short distance away. If you have managed to follow this path you should now turn right to a footpath sign on the left and a stone stile (the club house is on the right).

Once over the stile, strike diagonally to the left across the field, to a wooden stile in a wire fence. There is a stone stile in the wall a little further on. Turn right and the footpath back into Rose is on the opposite side of the road. This goes through a field of gorse, then through a small gate and into a field. In the far right corner the path emerges onto the lane through the centre of the hamlet of Rose. Turn right, then left, retracing the route back down the track between the two white houses, with the water pump next to the wall. The track ends at St Piran's Round and the start of the walk.

# 15. Holywell – the Wildflower Walk

**Route:** Holywell – Cubert Common – Cubert Barrow – Porth Joke – Kelsey Head Cliff Castle (remains) – The Kelseys – Cave and St Cuthbert's Well (optional) – Holywell.

**Distance:** 3½ miles

**Time:** 1¾ hours

**Terrain:** Easy. The walk is almost evenly divided between coast, common and sand dunes.

**Refreshments:** Holywell

**Access:** Holywell is situated at the end of a minor road which can be reached via the A3075, north of Goonhavern. The village is approximately three miles north of Perranporth, along the coast.

**Maps:** Ordnance Survey Explorer 104 Redruth and St Agnes, Ordnance Survey Landranger 200.

Holywell has, appropriately enough, two ancient holy wells. However, neither is directly on this route. St Cuthbert's Well is considered to be one of the most impressive in the county, occupying a mysterious calcified cave on the beach, which can only be accessed at low tide. For this reason it can be included as an optional detour. Even without such excitements, walking in this area, most of which is owned by the National Trust, is extremely rewarding due to the diversity of landscape and the variety of habitats. It is particularly good for wild flowers, with some rarities, such as the prickly poppy, flourishing here. In addition, a Bronze Age burial mound, an Iron Age cliff castle and an ancient enclosed common are also en route, making the walk the most rewarding stroll on this section of the north coast.

The start of the walk is in the car park at the end of the road through the village. From here, turn right up the road, then turn left opposite the public toilets, passing the stores and the café. At the choice of footpaths, take the path on the right, marked with a yellow arrow. This easily followed route heads up into the dunes, bearing to the right.

Although not a designated nature reserve like the dunes at Perranporth, this dune land is also home to a wide variety of plants, especially wild flowers, such as the pretty blue sea holly.

Soon a crossroads in the paths comes into view. The entrance to the golf course is through the metal gate, so follow the path which climbs up on the left. From here, look back towards the sea for some good views of the twin Gull Rocks on the west side of the bay. Cross over a wooden stile, leaving the dunes behind. The area on the left is part of the Kelseys, which will be explored a little further on. A few minutes later there is a gate on the right, with another yellow arrow. Go through the gate, then turn left, staying next to the stone hedge. This begins to curve away to the left slightly, but the path continues straight, heading towards a white house called The Commons. Just before this, a path strikes off to the left and a few metres further on, a wider track does the same. Continue to the track, but then turn right and walk for a short distance to Cubert Common.

This area of land is known as one of the few enclosed commons left in Britain, although it is no longer used for grazing livestock due to the large number of dogs exercised in the area. Not far down the track lies Cubert Barrow, an excellent example of a Bronze Age burial mound, and similar to others found all

*Holywell Bay*

over the county. It stands almost three metres high and well over thirty metres in diameter. Unlike many barrows, however, it has not been thoroughly excavated, and local legend warns that any attempt to tamper with it will result in terrible thunder storms.

Retrace the path to the white house, then continue along the track towards the sea. After a while the other, smaller path joins up and they curve down the valley and into a National Trust car park. On the left side of this there is a wooden gate, which is the start of the footpath down to Porth Joke.

This valley is full of colour and life, especially in spring and early summer. The graceful pink tamarisk is everywhere, with the gatekeeper butterfly lightly moving from bramble to bramble in the hedges. Closer to the stream, the highly unusual galingale can be found, a favourite with the cattle who occasionally come down from the common to shelter and drink. Also on the banks of the stream is wild watercress – do not be tempted to eat it, however, as the wild variety often contains parasites.

The path climbs up the cliff on the left side of the cove, emerging on the ancient, windswept cliff pastures of the Kelseys.

There are three pastures, enclosed by walls which were first mentioned in the Lanhydrock Atlas of 1694 and which probably predate that by some considerable time. With the exception of the outer wall, they are fairly high and built like those on Dartmoor which were used to keep royal deer out. They consist of a vertical approach on one side and a gentle slope on the other. The enclosures are still farmed in a traditional manner: planted with crops for part of the year, then grazed by cattle until ploughing.

This kind of habitat is home to different species from those in the valleys and dunes. Hares, adders and skylarks love the open grassland, as do certain varieties of wild flowers, such as thistles, of which there are ten different varieties in the area. Ancient fields bordered with hedges are the perfect habitat for other flowers such as yellow kidney vetch and wild poppies. The area around Holywell is home to the extremely rare prickly poppy, distinguished from its cousins by deeply lobed petals and club-shaped, bristly seed capsules. Birds such as the linnet love these 'weeds', and this pretty finch can often be spotted by its undulating flight and splash of pink on the breast in the summer. To the right, the large rock offshore is called The Chick and is home to various species of seabirds as well as seals, which can be seen basking in the sunshine from the cliffs.

Continue along the coast path and further on, at the very tip of the Kelsey

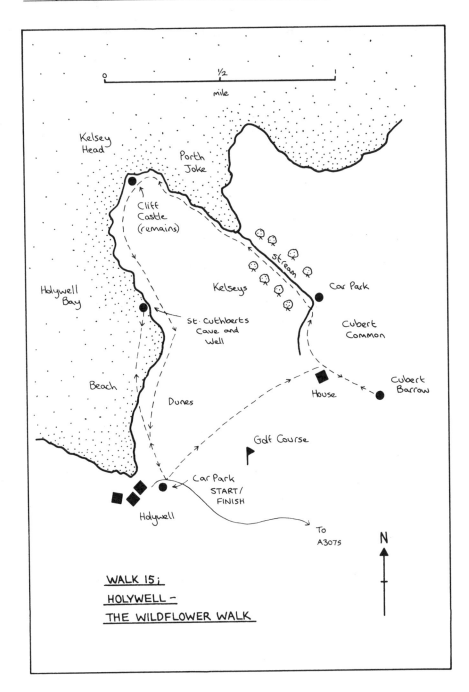

WALK 15;

HOLYWELL –

THE WILDFLOWER WALK

Head, there is an Iron Age cliff castle marked by two wooden waymark-ers.

It would be easy to spot without these as the remains of the outer ram-parts stand to over a metre, with the ditch almost five metres wide and run-ning for about 220 metres in a 'U' shape, pointing out to sea. The area it defended is about one hectare and would have been home for an entire com-munity, protected on one side by the sea and on the other by the huge ditch and rampart system.

Continue along the coast to a small gate which marks the route's re-entry onto the dunes. Follow the path, something which can be difficult in the ever shifting world of sand. If possible, keep on the boardwalks, as the sand dunes are a vulnerable environment. After a short distance, a wooden bridge should come into view, just to the right of the last houses in the village. Aim for this, then just before it there is a wide track which leads up to the left and emerges by the stores and the café.

To include a visit to St Cuthbert's cave and well, turn right off the dunes and onto the beach. It is imperative that a tide timetable is checked first, as the cave is only accessible at low tide. It is about 10 to 15 minutes walk away on the eastern side of the beach, at the base of the cliff. Of the three cave entrances, St Cuthbert's is the third and furthest, with rough steps hewn into the rock leading up from the beach into the cave.

There are, in fact, two caves here: the first has a series of basins naturally formed in the putty-coloured rock; the next cave is smaller and above the first at the top of the steps. The largest of the basins in the larger cave is the well, holding about a foot of crystal clear water which reflects the greens and blues in the mineral-encrusted rock. The cave is a place so magical, it is not hard to see why people have believed in its curative properties for centu-ries. In former times, mothers brought sick children here on Ascension Day and passed them through the entrance from the upper cave into the water. Similarly, the well was said to cure cripples, who then left their crutches at the entrance as an offering – a practice with heavy overtones of pagan ritu-als, which is not surprising as most holy wells in Cornwall have such origins.

However, unlike many such wells, St Cuthbert did not live in a cell nearby. He was Prior of the abbey on Lindisfarne. After his death, the monks of the holy island took his remains with them when fleeing from the Danes. They landed in Holywell Bay and the relics accidentally touched the well, rendering it holy. This may or may not be the case, but as with all such wells, they were holy places before Christianity came and any curative properties they possess undoubtedly pre-date the attentions of the newer religion.

# 16. Padstow and Stepper Point

**Route:**       Padstow – Prideaux Place – Trevone Bay – Stepper Point
             – Doom Bar – St George's Cove – Padstow.

**Distance:**    7 miles

**Time:**        3½ hours

**Terrain:**     Easy. Mostly coastal walking with some sections on high,
             exposed cliffs which could be dangerous in strong winds.

**Refreshments:** Padstow and Trevone Bay in the summer months.

**Access:**      Padstow is on the A389, west of Wadebridge. For public
             transport details, see the end of the chapter.

**Maps:**        Ordnance Survey Explorer 106 and Ordnance Survey
             Landranger 200.

This fairly long walk covers a variety of landscapes: from high, black cliffs with unusual rock formations, to the broad, sandy sweep of Padstow estuary and the Doom Bar. This is a walk of colours, many of which are truly dramatic. Even on an overcast day, the sand of Draymer Bay and the water which covers it have a startling luminosity. Almost all the discoveries to be made on this walk are natural, and many, especially the wildflowers, are at their best in spring and early summer.

The walk starts in Padstow itself, from the car park on the harbour side.

This small, mainly medieval town has much to recommend it and can therefore become very busy with visitors in high summer. Another time when the town is full to bursting point is on May Day, when a traditional festival which probably has its origins in pre-Christian fertility rites is performed. The now famous 'hobby horse', with its fearsome mask, dances through the green-bedecked streets on the backs of two men, to the tune of the May Day song. It is preceded by the 'teazer', the two symbolising sun and the earth, their wild dance ensuring a fruitful summer and good harvest.

During the 6th century, St Petroc, an Irish missionary, landed here and founded a monastery, so giving his name to the town. The church which now stands at the centre is mostly 15th-century and there are some remnants of that first religious settlement. Outside the south porch door there is a small, four-holed cross made of Cornish elvan stone. Such crosses are also often called 'preaching crosses', and it is possible that St Petroc stood below it as he preached to the new converts. Also in the church grounds is the elegantly decorated shaft of what would have been a much larger cross, which is thought to have stood in the gateway to the original monastery.

The walk leaves the town by a side exit, passing Prideaux Place. From the harbour, turn 180 degrees and walk up the main road, past the post office. There are occasional signs for the manor house. Turn right at the fork, then again at the next, walking past the entrance to the Tropical Bird and Butterfly Gardens on Fentonluna Lane. At the T-junction, turn right and the beautiful Elizabethan manor of Prideaux Place is on the left.

It came into the hands of the family (who still live there) after the Dissolution of the Monasteries, when the Prior of Bodmin gave the house to his steward, Nicholas Prideaux. The house has several stone crosses in the grounds, but the public has no access. The house is open to visitors in the summer months, from Easter onwards. See the information section for details.

Retrace the route back to the T-junction and continue straight, walking along the side of the hotel. At the next junction turn right, then right again to follow a small lane past the back of the manor. A short distance later there is a footpath sign on the left. This crosses two fields. Head for the telegraph pole in the first, then to the stile in the hedge, then leave the next field through the buildings. Once on the road, turn right, then almost immediately left, down a track which crosses the neck of the peninsula.

At the end of the track, it passes a farm on the right, then goes through a gate on to a small lane. Turn left, swinging down to the east side of Trevone Bay. Follow the sign for the coastal path on the right. The rest of the walk is through sheep country and all dogs must be kept on leads. As the cliff curves to the right, there is an unusual natural phenomenon up the slight incline on the right.

The huge Round Hole is exactly that – an almost perfectly round crater in the ground, at the bottom of which the sea can be seen. It is the first of several such collapsed caves along this part of the coast and extreme care should be taken as their edges are far from stable.

This section of the route is clearly waymarked and crosses sheep-cropped turf and a protected area of maritime grassland which is cared for by the Countryside Commission and English Nature.

The flowers along this stretch can be truly stunning in the spring and early

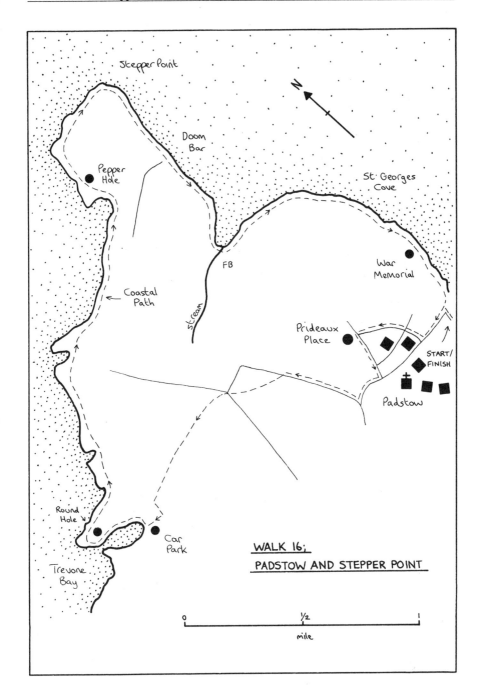

Stepper Point

Doom Bar

Pepper Hole

St Georges Cove

War Memorial

FB

Coastal Path

Stream

Prideaux Place

START/ FINISH

Padstow

Round Hole

Car Park

Trevone Bay

WALK 16;
PADSTOW AND STEPPER POINT

N

0          ½          1
mile

summer. The cliff tops are adorned not merely with the common sea pink, but with the bright yellow of kidney vetch and buttercups and with sea campion, sheep's sorrel and wild thyme adding to nature's spring parade. Birds are plentiful, too. Even though Padstow is quite far up the north coast, auks such as razorbills and guillemots can be found nesting in the area. The graceful, white fulmar also thrives here. Glorious colour is not restricted to flora and fauna. At Butter Hole the blues and purples of the rock glitter deceptively, oblivious to the many ships wrecked on its cruel teeth. At Stepper Point, with its first wonderful glimpse of Pentire Point and Doom Bar, the intriguing Pepperpot is now fenced off and dangerous to explore.

The coastal path continues to follow the edge of the cliffs and descends just past the Pepperpot, following the waymarkers.

Over to the left the Doom Bar shimmers, despite any lack of sunshine. Perhaps it is not surprising, therefore, to learn that there is a legend connected with it. The Bar is said to have been formed by the mermaid who guarded Padstow. One day, however, she was wounded by a young man and his crossbow. In retaliation, the mermaid withdrew her protection of the town and threw some sand at him, thereby creating the Bar.

The path emerges on to road by the coastguard station. Turn right here, then left, following the footpath sign down in front of some cottages. This again returns to the road, so turn left then left again, across a stile to the path which passes behind a house. Follow the path until the little detour inland to accommodate the Town Bar. After crossing the wooden bridge, the path comes to a T-junction. Turn right for a few metres, until another sign can be seen on the left, keeping the path running along the edge of the fields which border the sand. At the next, much shorter, detour inland, the pretty cove of St George lies on the left, down some stone steps.

There is a well here dedicated to the saint of the same name. It is no more than a spring which flows from a rock which the saint is said to have struck with his foot. Locals say it never dries up, but I couldn't find it to verify the story. It is located slightly inland from the cove and the path to it is hopelessly overgrown.

The path now widens out, forming part of a popular short walk from the town centre up to the cove. A short distance later, it reaches the town's war memorial. From here, several paths span out. Keep to the one on the left and it will eventually emerge on the west side of the quay. Walk around this to return to the car park.

In doing so you will pass the 15th-century Abbey House and the Court House of Sir Walter Raleigh on the North Quay.

# 17. Boscastle and the Valency Valley

**Route:** Boscastle – Valency Valley – Minster Church – Bottreaux Castle (remains) – Forrabury Church and Cross – The Stitches – Willapark Cliff Castle (remains) – Harbour – Boscastle.

**Distance:** 3½ miles

**Time:** 1¾ hours

**Terrain:** Moderate. The walk is a mixture of woodland, farmland and coastal paths. The route includes two steep ascents, but all paths are in regular use and are easily discernible.

**Refreshments:** Boscastle and Boscastle Harbour

**Access:** Boscastle is on the B3266, north of Camelford and the A39.

**Maps:** Ordnance Survey Explorer 111.

This is a wonderful little walk, packed full with things to see. Boscastle has escaped the rampant commercialism of Tintagel, just a few miles down the coast, and has much more to offer. The village and much of the surrounding area is owned by the National Trust and is thereby allowed to retain its beauty and charm. The Valency Valley is likewise protected, as is its thriving wildlife. Spring is probably the best time of year to visit this fertile crack in the severe face of the north coast, but each season gives Boscastle's rare corner a different appeal.

The walk starts in the only car park in Boscastle. Go through the village towards the harbour and the car park is on the right, next to the North Cornwall Visitor Centre. The beautiful Valency Valley is also on the right, and a small wooden gate leading on to the path is situated at the opposite end of the car park from the visitor centre.

This valley is famous thanks to its literary connections. The writer and poet Thomas Hardy came to the church of St Juliot at the head of the valley in 1870, as the representative of an architectural firm engaged to restore the church. It was here that he met Emma Gifford and their romance blossomed on the banks of the River Valency. After his initial visit, Hardy returned and their relationship developed, Emma encouraging him to give up architecture for literature. This he did, and they married in 1874. Hardy's time in this part of Cornwall and his relationship with the vicar's young sister- in- law greatly influenced his third novel *A Pair Of Blue Eyes*, which was published in 1873.

The valley runs inland from the harbour, a fertile seam in a windswept landscape. Spring and early summer are the best times to explore the area, when wild flowers cover the ground between the oak, ash and hazel trees, providing food for butterflies such as the bright yellow brimstone and the small pearl-bordered fritillary. This delicate flash of silver and brown can be seen darting across woodland glades in June and July. The valley is also home to larger creatures such as foxes and badgers, whilst the river provides food for herons and even otters.

**Follow the fairly wide path along the northern (left) bank of the river, until it reaches a large, wooden footbridge. A footpath sign indicates the route to Minster Church on the opposite bank. Cross the stream and follow the path, which makes a rapid ascent up the side of the valley.**

Magnificent views across the valley and down to the sea are a reward for completing the most strenuous part of the route. The path then meanders down through the trees to the beautiful but eerie Minster Church, enclosed by the sides of the valley and surrounded by trees, amongst which headstones stand in silent watchfulness. Legend has it that this part of Peter's Wood is haunted and this is not difficult to believe. Monks from the monastery which stood here until the 15th century are said to wander through the trees and the once terraced gardens.

There has been a religious settlement on this site since around AD500 when Madryn, a Welsh princess, settled here to pray and heal the sick. The holy well associated with her lay north of the church, but was in ruins by the 14th century and almost nothing remains of it now. The present church dates from 1150, although it was restored in 1507 and again in 1869, when the roof fell in. The best time to discover this, the most unusual church in the book, is during early spring when daffodils carpet the whole glade, dispelling the slightly oppressive atmosphere.

**Follow the metalled path up to the right, to a wooden gate leading on to a country lane. Turn right, then right again at the fork. Soon after this the road curves to the left and there is a footpath sign straight ahead, leading**

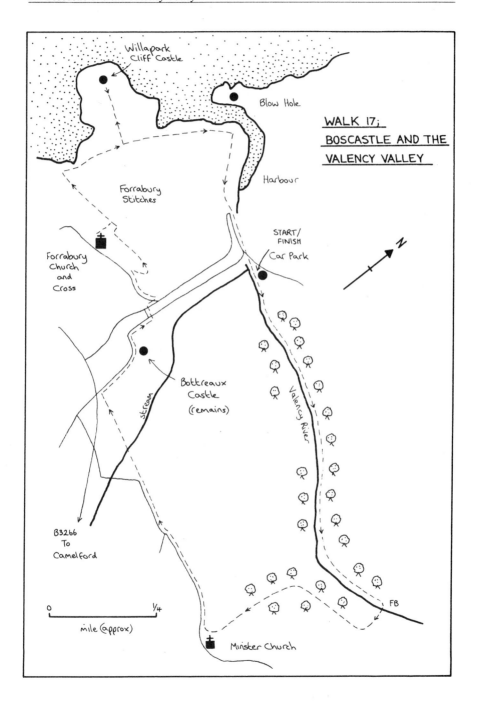

Willapark
Cliff Castle

Blow Hole

WALK 17;
BOSCASTLE AND THE
VALENCY VALLEY

Harbour

Forrabury
Stitches

START/
FINISH
Car Park

N

Forrabury
Church
and
Cross

Bottreaux
Castle
(remains)

Stream

Valency River

B3266
To
Camelford

0                     ¼

mile (approx)

FB

Minster Church

over a stone stile into a field. Cross this, aiming for the bottom left corner
by the buildings. A wooden gate opens onto a yard between a cottage
and a pond (inhabited by relatively non-aggressive geese). Turn right
and walk across the yard, following the signs up the track straight ahead,
which runs between some more houses before emerging on a road. Turn
right and follow it downhill.

> This is the road which runs down through the old part of Boscastle, a village
> which owes its existence not only to the natural harbour, but also the de
> Botterell family. Nicholas de Botterell fought with William the Conqueror
> and built his castle on a spur overlooking the valley and harbour. The remains
> of Bottreaux Castle are on the right of this old road through the village cen-
> tre.

A small, metalled path with a red sign prohibiting dogs indicates the way
up to the steep, grassy slope, now equipped with picnic tables.

Retrace the path back to the road and turn right, continuing along the
street and past the post office. Just after the Londis grocery shop, the
road forks. Take the road on the left, which climbs up to the new road
through the village. Cross this and continue up Forrabury Hill. As the road
curves to the right, there is a footpath sign to the coast also on the right.
Follow this up through some trees and through a small gate to some farmland.

> It will become immediately obvious that these are no ordinary fields. They are
> organised in long, narrow rectangles, bounded by low banks and provide a
> rare example of an ancient Celtic field system. The 'stitches' are used in the
> traditional manner, growing corn or potatoes in the summer and as common
> pasture during the winter months. This system has been retained thanks to
> the ownership of the National Trust, which rents the land to local farmers.
> The uncultivated banks between the stitches are covered in many varieties
> of wild flowers during the summer months, and each stitch has been shown
> in surveys by Plymouth University to be ecologically different. All this makes
> the Forrabury Stitches a highly significant piece of ancient and natural his-
> tory, so take care to stick to the footpath which runs along the edge.

The path stays on the right of the hedge which borders the church of St
Symphorian of Forrabury. There is a small gate in the hedge which leads
into the churchyard.

> The church is very early Norman, but evidence of this remains only in the nave
> and the south transept as the church underwent extensive restoration in
> 1867, a renovation which unfortunately led to the destruction of the medie-

val oak benches. On the south side of the churchyard is an early Christian wheel cross, standing to over a metre and a half in height. It was apparently once used as a gatepost as there are three holes on the back. The tower of this church has an unusual weather vane in the shape of a fish. It is said to act as a reminder of the close connections with the fishing industry, important, of course, all over Cornwall, but it would be appropriate to any Christian church.

**Return to the path along the edge of the Stitches and continue towards the sea. This path reaches a T-junction with the coastal path. Turn right along this, towards the impressive promontory of Willapark, with its white lookout.**

The path passes the entrance to the promontory on the left, which was probably also the entrance to the Iron Age cliff castle which once made use of the site's natural defences. All that remains of the castle now is a ditch and rampart, the latter standing to just under two metres in places, but still running the whole length of the neck of the promontory. A path leads up to the lookout which, at 300ft (100 metres) above sea level, provides stunning views of both the coastline and inland.

**Return to the coastal path and continue north, descending fairly rapidly into Boscastle Harbour.**

If this is done an hour either side of low tide, the lucky walker may see a huge waterspout from the blow hole called Devil's Bellows on Penally point, opposite.

**The path follows the length of the harbour as it reaches inland.**

The original inner harbour was built by Sir Richard Grenville in 1584 and became, thanks to its being the only harbour for 40 miles of coastline, a major bustling port. Schooners and ketches brought coal and limestone from Wales and many other general goods from Bristol, returning with cargoes of slate, china clay, corn and tanning bark. It is hard to believe now, but Boscastle was once the main port for all of Launceston's maritime trade, most of the ships being towed into the narrow, winding harbour and manoeuvred by local oarsmen. Boscastle's decline as a commercial port began in 1893 with the arrival of the first railway to reach north Cornwall.

**Follow the steps down from the coastal path to the harbour side, opposite the Witchcraft Museum. Turn right and walk past the phone box and across the road, back to the car park and the start of the walk.**

# 18. Hawker Country – Morwenstow and Higher Sharpnose Point

**Route:** Morwenstow and Church – St John's Well – Henna Cliff – St Morwenna's Well – Hawker's Hut – Higher Sharpnose Point – Tidna Shute Valley – Bush Inn – Morwenstow.

**Distance:** 3 miles

**Time:** 2 hours

**Terrain:** Challenging. There are several climbs and difficult descents, some close to the edges of cliffs, so the walk is probably not suitable for very young children. However, any reasonably fit adult with a head for heights would have no problems.

**Refreshments:** Rectory Tea Rooms by the church, and the Bush Inn at Crosstown.

**Access:** Follow the signs for Morwenstow off the A39 north of Bude.

**Maps:** Ordnance Survey Landranger 109 and Ordnance Survey Explorer 126.

For anyone unfamiliar with this often neglected part of Cornwall, this walk will come as something of a shock. Just a few miles north of the gentle shores of the Camel estuary and the sandy beaches of Bude, lies Cornwall's most impressive coastline. This section of the north coast, which is almost in Devon, has been designated a Heritage Coast by the Countryside Commission, and with good reason. The unassuming hills and wooded combes of the area suddenly rise to a height of 450ft (144 metres) as they meet the sea which has carved the rock into the sharp ridges so lethal to passing shipping. Walking in this area is a breathtaking experience in both senses of the word, yet the drama of the coast is contrasted with gentle woodland, which is covered in flowers and filled with birdsong in the spring.

This part of Cornwall is known as Hawker Country, after the parson of the parish from 1834 to 1874. He was thought of as an eccentric, but in reality was a highly intelligent, creative man, who found himself in a remote parish, far from the stimulation of his peers. He is credited with several achievements, including the introduction of the Christian version of the pagan Harvest Festival in 1843, and for writing some notable poetry. He was also horrified at the fate of so many ships in the area and often went into the sea himself to save drowning sailors, giving those he failed to rescue a Christian burial in the churchyard.

The latter has several points of interest. In the Lych House (from the Saxon for corpse) next to the main gate, the bodies of sailors were laid out prior to burial. Next to this is a Celtic cross, said to have been taken from Roughtor on Bodmin Moor, although there is a possibility that it could be a 19th-century copy. The initials of Hawker's wife are carved into the front of the cross. Also of note in the churchyard is the white figurehead of the Scottish 500-ton brig *Caledonia* which sank in 1842, a tragedy which only one man survived.

The walk starts in the informal car park between the churchyard and the Rectory Tearooms. There are a multitude of footpath signs here. Follow those on the far right (if standing facing the church) down the track which curves around to the left, towards the vicarage. After a short distance there is a National Trust sign on the right, indicating the short permissive path to St John's Well in a garden.

The well is housed in a small building, with a wooden door which is kept padlocked and a Latin cross positioned on top of the foremost gable. The well itself has been in use since 1296 and its water is still used today for baptisms, which always take place in the Saxon font in the church. The font dates from around AD950 and was found by Norman builders when working on the new church. The water from the spring in the well is said to be especially pure. Parson Hawker never drank any other!

Opposite the National Trust sign there is a large, wooden gate leading into the churchyard. Go through here and follow the path to the stone stile on the right, between the outbuilding and the vicarage. Follow the path between the buildings as marked with yellow arrows.

On the left is the vicarage built by Parson Hawker after the previous one was found to be uninhabitable. The profusion of distinctive chimneys tells us something of the originality of this poet and philanthropist. Three of the chimneys are based on Cornish church towers, two on Oxford colleges, where Hawker won an important poetry prize, and one on his mother's tombstone.

Ignore the first path indicated on the left, which is a permissive route along the valley floor. Cross the wooden footbridge and continue up the side of the combe (as valleys are known in this part of Cornwall) until the trees end. Here, there is a waymarker indicating the path on the left to Henna Cliff. From this superb vantage point comes the first taste of some of the fabulous views on this walk and some of the challenges. Descend down the combe on the left and cross the wooden footbridge, following the coastal footpath.

On the right as the path starts to climb are the remains of the well of St Morwenna, now entirely inaccessible. Morwenna, after whom the parish is named, was a Welsh princess who came to this part of Cornwall in the 6th century, choosing a new home which had views of her native country on a fine day. It was in this direction that she faced when she died in the arms of her brother, St Nectan.

Do not be deterred by the steepness of the path here as the walker is rewarded with the first outstanding view of Higher Sharpnose Point directly ahead. From this level also, the sharp black teeth of the Bude Formation – rocks which have ended the lives of so many sailors over the centuries – can be seen at low tide.

**Take care on this section of path** as it passes very close to the crumbling edge of the cliff. After a short distance, there comes into view another National Trust sign, pointing this time to Hawker's Hut, known as the smallest of all Trust properties.

The hut is built out of driftwood and is where the parson sat and smoked opium, whilst writing poetry and watching for ships. Hawker was probably the best of the minor Victorian poets. His two most famous works are *The Ballad of Western Men*, now the Cornish national anthem, and a poem entitled *Quest of the Sangraal*, which appeared in print five years before Tennyson's *Holy Grail* and was preferred to the work of the Poet Laureate by many. Tennyson himself visited this part of Cornwall, when he came to see Tintagel. He met Hawker by accident and subsequently stayed with the parson, Hawker lending Tennyson several rare manuscripts and books on the history and legends of the area.

At the next hedge to meet the coastal path, there is a path back up to the church. Ignore this and continue down the side of the combe. On the left is Tidna Shute Valley. On the right there is a small, wooden footbridge and a footpath up to Sharpnose Point.

This small detour and the climb involved are well worth the effort as the views from this curious rocky promontory are truly breathtaking. From the

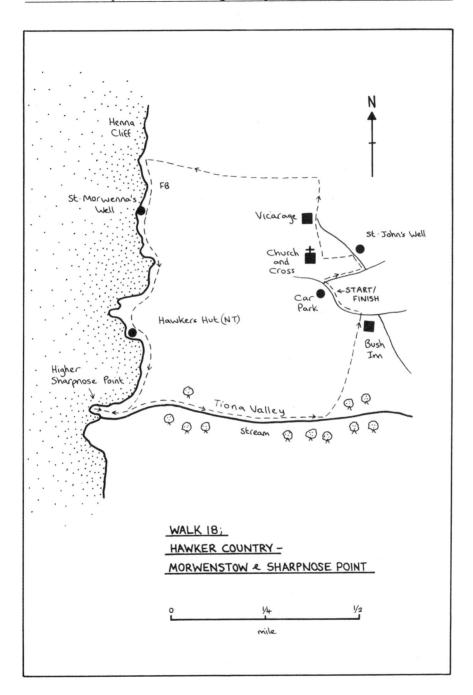

WALK 18;
HAWKER COUNTRY –
MORWENSTOW & SHARPNOSE POINT

*Hawker's Hut*

end one can look back at this savage coastline, with its sharp rock and crumbling cliffs, and on a clear day, Lundy Island and even the hills of Wales are visible to the north-east.

Retrace the path to the Countryside Commission sign at the previous intersection of paths. Follow the path which runs along the valley floor, with the stream on the right and the fence on the left. After the first field there is a stile and then the path enters the Tidna Valley Woods.

Tough, cliff-hugging flowers give way to more delicate varieties such as foxglove and yellow iris, whilst the woodland itself provides shelter to all kinds of bird and animal life, a startling contrast to the drama of cliffs and sea ten minutes away.

Most maps indicate the path crossing the stream. However, at present, it stays on the left bank, passing three small, wooden bridges on the right. Just past the last of these, the path swings sharply to the left and climbs a bank via some steps which lead to a stile. Cross this and walk directly up the field to the next stile amongst some trees.

Once over this, walkers will be pleasantly surprised to find themselves in the garden of the Bush Inn, an old smuggling haunt.

Go through the gate on the left of the pub and cross the grass to the road. Turn left and follow the road as it curves around, passing the sign for the Rectory Tea Rooms, and heading back into Morwenstow and the start of the walk.

# Useful Information

**Transport in the North Coast Area:** The nearest main line train stations to points included in this section are Redruth and Bodmin Parkway. For all rail enquires, call 0345 484950. Local bus services are adequate, only Walk 18 may cause serious problems. For services in north and mid-Cornwall, call 01208 79898. For services to the St Agnes area from Redruth, call 01209 719988 and from Truro, call 01872 273453.

**Other Information:** Prideaux Place, Padstow, open Easter – mid-October, or all year by appointment. Call 01841 532411.

**Tourist Information Centres:** Newquay, Marcus Hill, 01637 871345; Bude, Cresent Car Park, 01288 354240; Boscastle, Cobweb Car Park, 01840 250010; Padstow, North Quay, 01841 533449; Perranporth 01872 573368.

**Youth Hostels:** Palace Stable, Boscastle, 01840 250287; Tregannan, Treyarnon, Padstow, 01841 520322.

# The
# South Coast

*Duloe Stone Circle: see walk 23*

---

# 19. Trelissick and the Carrick Roads

---

**Route:**          Trelissick Nature Trail – Fort (remains) – Roundwood
                    Quay – Cowlands Creek – Punch Bowl and Ladle Inn –
                    Come-To-Good Quaker House – Trelissick.

**Time:**           2 hours

**Distance:**       4½ miles

**Terrain:**        Easy. Mostly woodland and some farmland.
                    Well-maintained paths.

**Refreshments:** Punch and Ladle pub, Penelewey (on route); Trelissick
                    Gardens (March to Christmas).

**Access:**         If travelling by car, turn off the A30 at Playing Place onto
                    the B3289. Park in the lay-by on the left at the top of
                    Trevilla Hill. The footpath is down a track marked on the
                    left. Buses to Trelissick go from Truro. See end of chapter
                    for details.

**Map:**            Explorer 105, Landranger 204 Truro and Falmouth.

---

This is a very pleasant walk around some of the gentlest and most picturesque scenery in Cornwall. It is also possibly one of the most varied in terms of sites of interest. The walk includes some of the Trelissick Nature Trail, but avoids the main car park and gardens, although these are less than a quarter of a mile further down the road from the start of the walk. The house itself is not open to the public, but the parkland can become very busy in the summertime, when a fee for parking in the grounds is also charged.

On the same side of the road as the lay-by is a footpath sign pointing down a track which descends into woodland. When this reaches a stream, there are two small, wooden gates on the right. Go through the one on the nearside of the stream. This part of the walk is on National Trust property, following part of a nature trail through the managed woodland here.

'Tref-gwlesyk', meaning 'farmstead of the leader' in Cornish, first came into

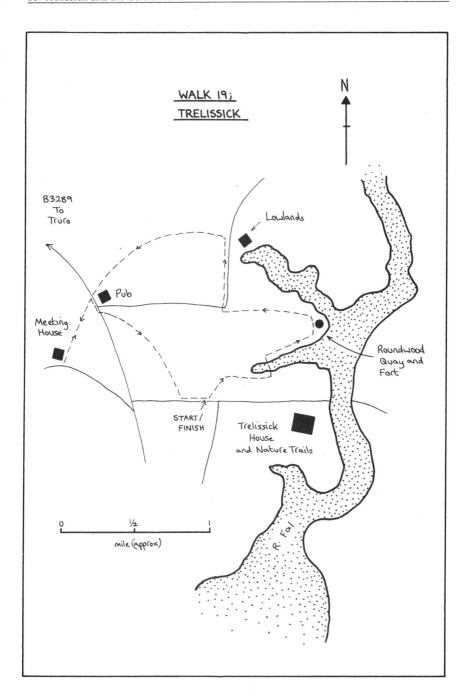

WALK 19;
TRELISSICK

N

B3289
To
Truro

Lowlands

Pub

Meeting
House

Roundwood
Quay and
Fort

START/
FINISH

Trelissick
House
and Nature Trails

0    ½    1
mile (approx)

R. Fal

being in 1750, when the Lawrence family built the mansion on the site of a farm. It was designed by the architect Edmund Davy, grandfather of Sir Humphrey Davy. The house and grounds were extended and improved by the Daniell family, who had made their fortune in tin mining in the 19th century. For most of its history, the parkland around the estate has been conscientiously managed, leaving the wonderful and varied gardens and woodland which are open to the public. These include sub-tropical plants and many different tree varieties.

The route now goes through Namphillow wood, which was planted in the 1830s with oak and pine for commercial use. At the head of Lamouth Creek, there is a wooden bridge. Cross this, turn right and follow the path along the edge of the water through Lambsclose Plantation.

This is another managed woodland. It was planted with sessile oak, distinguished from English oak by its less distinctive lobing and the acorns which grow directly on the twig in pairs. The wood was then coppiced, an ancient practice used to produce thin switches of wood for fencing and tool handles, whilst the bark was used in the tanning process.

The creek on the right is, in fact, an ancient stream bed, which was drowned when the ice caps melted and the seas rose. Like much of the River Fal and the Carrick Roads, low tide reveals mud flats with very deep creeks in the centre. These inlets and shallow waters provide excellent hunting grounds for ornithologists as the area is home to many birds, including kingfishers, redshanks, greenshanks, oystercatchers and black tailed godwits. Across the creek, Stitches Plantation can be seen. This was replanted in the 1960s with beech and larch, but was originally sub-divided field strips dating from the medieval period.

A few metres before the path descends into Roundwood Quay there is an Iron Age fort at the end of the promontory. It is on the left of the path.

Remains of the ditches and ramparts can still be seen, the latter up to around 3 metres in height. The two parallel banks span the neck of the promontory, with entrances on the western side. Inside, there is an oval enclosure. It can clearly be seen why the site was chosen – it has a natural vantage point over this part of the Carrick Roads where the Fal and the Truro rivers converge.

The quay itself has been used as a departure point for shipments of tin and copper since the 18th century. The Chacewater Copper Company built wharves, smelting and refining facilities. By the early part of the 19th century, however, its role had been superseded by the railway which ran from Gwennap mines to Devoran (remains of which can still be seen in Devoran, including some of the buildings which are entirely intact). Yet by the end of the century, it was back in use as a site for shipbuilding. Indeed, a sawpit can still be seen in the centre of the quay.

Roundwood Quay looks out across the Carrick Roads and the River Fal. Although 'Karrek Roode' means 'rocky harbour', the river is, in fact, both Britain's largest deep water harbour and the third largest natural harbour in the world. It is still a shock, however, to emerge from peaceful woodland on to the banks of a calm river and confront an immense wall of steel: the hull of one of many ocean-going vessels from all over the world which come up the 24-metre deep channel, totally dwarfing the natural surroundings.

From the quay, go left, through the large, wooden gate, and follow the track through the houses. This leads to a T-junction with a lane. Turn right and walk down into Cowlands Creek, which is a pretty and secluded hamlet. At the very head of the creek on the left is a footpath sign, pointing inland. Follow this through the woods, until it emerges in a field. Cross this, aiming for the gate in the hedge on the right, on the far side (but not in the part where the field narrows ). This leads into a lane by a house. Go through the main gate on to the driveway, then bear left (there are some waymarkers with yellow arrows to guide walkers through this part).

As the path opens out into fields, there are some excellent views across farmland. It's hard to believe this is the same county of cruel cliffs and high moorland, it could almost be the Home Counties.

In the last field, the path cuts diagonally across the field to the farm, passing to the left of the house. Where the track swings right, however, the route goes on, directly across the field opposite, with more good views down to the left. The path crosses a stile in the far hedge and goes by the back of some houses before emerging on to the road. On the left, a few metres along the road, is the 14th-century pub called the Punch Bowl and Ladle which serves food and has many cosy corners in which to take a well-earned rest!

Opposite the pub is a lane, which goes down to the rather oddly-named Come To Good.

This, however, is a corruption of the Cornish 'Cwm-ty-quite', meaning 'house of the combe in the woods'. On the right is a thatched Quaker Meeting House, built in 1710. It is open during the day, except for the organ loft. Very little light comes in through the tiny, leaded panes, but the simple room is one of tranquillity.

Return up the lane to Penelewey. Turn right and continue to the first road on the left past the pub. On the corner there is a footpath sign, which indicates a path down through woods and past houses. It emerges on a road. Turn right, then left, then right, following the footpath sign at the end of the road, which leads into fields. The stile is in the diagonal corner of the first field and the second has a stile by the house in the far corner (not through the gate on to the road). Turn left along the road and in a few hundred metres you reach the lay-by and the start of the walk.

*Round Houses, Veryan: walk 20*

# 20. Veryan and Nare Head

**Route:** Veryan Round Houses – Nare Head – Carne Barrow – Veryan Castle (remains) – Veryan.

**Distance:** 4 miles

**Time:** 2 hours

**Terrain:** Easy. Mostly farmland, with some coastal walking which has one slightly steeper section.

**Refreshments:** Veryan

**Access:** Take the signposted turning off the A3078 south of Tregony. Public transport may be a problem. See end of chapter for details.

**Maps:** Ordnance Survey Explorer 105 Falmouth and Mevagissey, Landranger 204.

Veryan is an extremely attractive village which has managed to re-sist the vulgarities of mass tourism to a large extent. Nare Head is also relatively under-visited (and underrated) by these standards. Add to this such sites of interest as the unusual 19th-century round houses in the village centre and one of the country's largest burial mounds, and it becomes clear that there is much to recommend this walk to almost anyone.

The walk starts in the leafy and genteel centre of Veryan. If one ignores the ill-advised but mercifully small development of bungalows on the edge of the village, then one could almost expect Miss Marple to emerge from beneath a thatched porch. All roads lead to the centre and this is where the church lies, surrounded by trees and bordered by a small stream. It has an unusual dedication – to St Symphorian – and is known as the final resting place of Admiral Kempe, an explorer who travelled with Cook.

From the centre, walk up the hill on the road to Pendower. After a few me-tres the road comes to some of the white-painted round houses which made Veryan famous.

Two of the total five flank this part of the road. The houses were built in the 19th century by Jeremiah Trist, who adopted a plan for a labourer's cottage published in Worgan's Agricultural Survey of 1811. Despite the rumours that their shape is to deter the devil from lurking in corners, the original reasons seem to have been more practical, including making them easier to clean! The houses were originally to be roofed with slate, but thatch was cheaper to obtain and the houses were erected for less than £50 each.

Continue a few metres further down the road to the footpath sign on the left, which runs up the side of a playing field before opening out on farmland. The path is easy to discern and crosses three fields, using stiles. The final field has a stile in the far left corner, by the buildings. Once on the lane, turn left for a short distance, to the footpath on the right. This is marked only by an easily missed stile consisting of stones jutting out of the wall – a form favoured in this area. Stick to the left hedge in both this and the next field, then keep the hedge on the right for the next two, before emerging on to another lane.

Turn right and follow the lane south, in the direction of Nare Head. Three cattle grids are crossed, the first a few hundred metres before a small National Trust car park. At this point, several paths radiate out across the countryside. The route to the headland, however, is across the next cattle grid and along the track. At the third and final grid, the track ends in gorse, with the cliff edge and a good view of Gull Rock on the left. Continue straight ahead and the path through the gorse will become clear. The main route stays on the outer edge of the headland, just inside the gorse, but there is a small track out to the Head itself.

This offers excellent views across Gerrans Bay, with the Roseland Peninsula on the right and the Lizard Peninsula beyond that. It is odd that a view such as this should be so neglected – which, of course, makes it all the more pleasant for those who do find it!

Waymarkers show the way down the western side of the Head, descending quickly to Tregagle's Hole.

This section of the walk offers plenty to see much closer to hand. Violets line the path every summer and, closer to the edge of the cliff, the valiant trefoil, a member of the clover family, clings to life despite the salty gales and the attentions of sheep.

Tregagle's Hole is marked by an abandoned cottage and a small footbridge. This unfortunate character is said to have risen from his grave to seek retribution from a man who wronged him. As punishment for this, his spirit is doomed to making a truss of sand, bound with ropes of sand, until the Day of Judgement. It is said his cries of frustration can be heard on stormy nights.

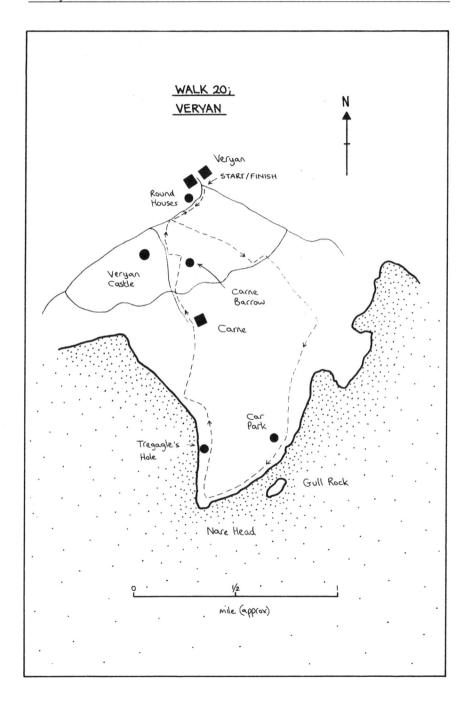

WALK 20;
VERYAN

N

Veryan
START/FINISH
Round
Houses

Veryan
Castle

Carne
Barrow

Carne

Car
Park

Tregagle's
Hole

Gull Rock

Nare Head

0          ½          1

mile (approx)

On a more cheerful note, there is plenty of life here, mainly in the form of wild flowers, including the ever present kidney vetch, as well as sea plantain and elder, which has adopted one side of the hut. There is plenty of bird life also, such as the little yellow hammer, with its distinctive patch of colour on the head and breast.

Cross the footbridge here and continue along the coastal path, crossing two small stone stiles. After the second, the path forks. Take the one on the right, which swings inland. At the next junction, go right again, following the signpost for Carne. Once in the hamlet and on the lane, go left, past the post box in the wall and past the road to the right. As the road makes a 90-degree turn to the left, continue straight on, over the large stile and into the field. Directly ahead is Carne Barrow.

At over 34 metres (100ft) in diameter and 21ft high, this is the largest Bronze Age barrow in Cornwall. Legend states that this is the final resting place of King Gereint, one of the last kings of Cornwall, who fought the invading Saxons. Gereint is named in the ancient Welsh tale of *Mabinogion* as 'son of Erbin', a god of the underworld. The rather fantastic tale of Gereint's death comes from the *Life of St Teilo*, written in the 12th century. Teilo lived in the 6th century and is said to have stayed at Gereint's court, located at Dingerein Castle, a few miles from here. He was called to hear the king's deathbed confession, before the king was, buried in the mound in a golden boat with silver oars.

Sadly, an excavation carried out in 1855 by the Reverend John Adams found no evidence of this wonderful story. However, the outer edges were used as a repository of ashes long after the barrow's construction. This suggests that it does contain the sacred remains of some ancient king in the central stone cist, somebody who reigned thousands of years before Gereint and who was so important, later remains were placed as close as possible to the original cist.

Five hundred metres north-west of here are the scant remains of Veryan Castle, lying in a field which can be seen from the road on the left. The enclosure, which measures up to 55 metres in diameter, has the usual ditch and rampart system of defence, unusually cut into the side of a hill.

From the entrance to the barrow, strike diagonally for the left hedge, where there is a stile on to the road. To see Veryan Castle, continue walking along the road until it can be seen on the left. Otherwise, the route continues to the right after the stile, and almost immediately over another stile into the next field. Stay with the hedge on the right, then turn right on to the lane and back into the village.

# 21. Gorran Haven and Dodman Point

| | |
|---|---|
| **Route:** | Gorran Haven Village – St Just Church – Dodman Point – Iron Age Fort (remains) – Gorran Haven. |
| **Distance:** | 4½ miles |
| **Time:** | 2¼ hours |
| **Terrain:** | Easy to moderate. Some short coastal sections are fairly steep and pass close to the edge of the cliffs. |
| **Refreshments:** | Gorran Haven |
| **Access:** | The simplest route is to take the B3273 to Mevagissey, then follow the signposts to Gorran Haven. If approaching from the opposite direction, the closest main road is the A3087 at Tregony to the west, from where many small country lanes criss-cross the countryside around Veryan Bay. Take a map! If using public transport, catch the #26/a from School Hill in Mevagissey. Services may be infrequent, see end of chapter for details. |
| **Maps:** | Ordnance Survey Explorer 105 Falmouth and Mevagissey, Ordnance Survey Landranger 204. |

The east side of the Roseland Peninsula from St Mawes to Mevagissey seems strangely neglected sometimes in comparison to the volume of visitors which descends on the surfing beaches of the north coast and the remote beauty of Penwith. Gorran Haven is no exception. Perhaps it has something to do with the extraordinary difficulty involved in reaching the village, especially if one is travelling from the west. Whatever the reason, the visitor is generously rewarded with a magnificent coastline, a rich history and wonderful beaches. This walk offers but a small taste of what the area has to offer.

The walk starts at the main car park in the centre of Gorran Haven. From here, turn left down the main road into the village centre.

*The origins of Gorran Haven are in farming and fishing, the earliest known* record of which dates back to 1270. At that time, the most powerful and wealthy family was that of the Bodrugans, who remained prominent until the late 15th century, when the last of the family died in exile after supporting a rebellion against King Henry VII.

**Continue along this road to the public toilets. On the opposite side of the road there is a small alley on the left, marked public footpath. This is one of the oldest parts of the village. Turn left as the alley emerges on a lane, then right for the church of St Just.**

This church is, in fact, a chapel of ease to St Gorran parish church and has had something of an uncertain history. There seems little doubt that there has been a chapel on this site since the days of the Celtic church in the early Dark Ages. Nothing of this structure remains, but many churches in Cornwall occupy the sites of earlier chapels or the cells of saints. St Just is certainly one of those Celtic saints who maintained the flame of Christianity in the face of the heathen Saxon invaders and the absence of the departed Romans. St Just himself probably came from Wales, where he is associated with St Gwrin at Llanwrin, a name on which 'Goran' is a variation.

The present structure dates mainly from the 15th century and owes its existence to Sir Henry Bodrugan, although it was suggested by Canon Adams in his history of the church that Sir Henry had something of an ulterior motive. Many Celtic chapels built by hermits and saints were used later in the middle ages as lighthouses. Much of the family wealth of the Bodrugans came from trade across the sea. Therefore, any light in the chapel would be a great aid to Sir Henry's ships. In the following centuries the church fell into disrepair and was even used as a fisherman's store, until a major restoration in 1885 by Piers St Aubyn.

**On leaving the church, walk east along the building to the edge of the harbour.**

From here there is a good view of the quay. This was built in 1885, the same year as the church refurbishment, although the earliest quay was built in 1585. Along with many subsequent quays, it was washed away by violent storms over the years.

**Turn right past the entrance to the beach and walk up Foxhole Lane on the left to the stile marked Vault Beach. Follow this path past a stone bench, keeping left at the fork as it rounds Maenese Point and the Dodman comes into view.**

The unusual name of 'Dodman' comes from the Cornish word 'tomen', mean-

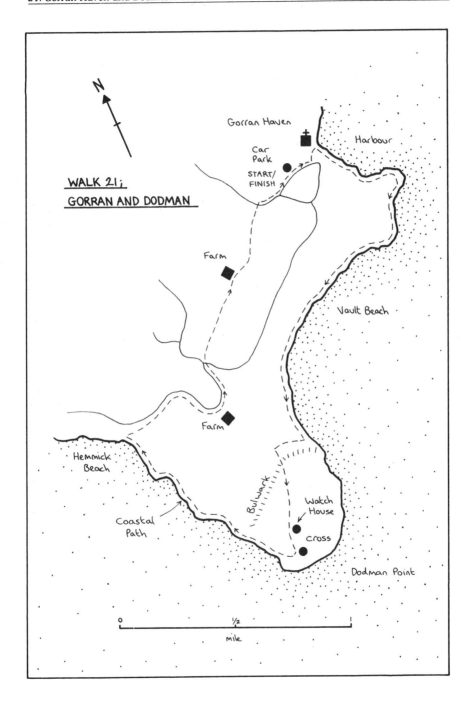

N

WALK 21;
GORRAN AND DODMAN

Gorran Haven

Car
Park
START/
FINISH

Harbour

Farm

Vault Beach

Farm

Hemmick
Beach

Bulwark

Watch
House

Cross

Coastal
Path

Dodman Point

0                          ½                          1
mile

ing 'bank' or 'dyke'. This will make perfect sense later in the walk as the path runs next to the massive fortifications of an Iron Age fort.

The path forks again here, so keep right, following the waymarker for the coastal path. Stick to this path, passing through a kissing gate and over a stile, before entering a small wood.

From here, part of the outer ramparts of the Iron Age cliff castle which once occupied this site can be seen.

The path runs over the end of an outer bank and continues to a crossroads in the paths. Take the path which makes a sharp right and swings round in an arc.

On the left is the massive bank known as the Bulwark, which stretches for an unbelievable 600 metres across the neck of the promontory. Measuring several metres in height despite erosion and agricultural damage, it is not hard to imagine how formidable an obstacle this would have been to anyone attempting to storm the fortification.

The number of such forts which still remain today gives us some indication of how uncertain and brutal life was in the immediate pre-Roman era. Almost all the large defensive works date from this period and many were re-used during the Dark Ages. Dodman is unusual, however, as no hut circles or other dwellings have been found inside the ramparts, only the remains of two burial mounds, which could have been built up to two thousand years earlier.

Cross the stile and go left along the farm track around the bank (the track on the right is a green lane to Penare Farm). After just a few metres, there is a path on the left which leads inside the site of the largest cliff castle in the county.

These twenty hectares, bordered by cruel cliffs and tumultuous seas, contain both the burial mounds and the remains of an ancient strip field system, although the pattern of much of this has been altered by farming over the intervening centuries.

The path leads directly south across the fort and is easily discernible. Go through a kissing gate and past the tiny 19th-century watchouse, used as an Admiralty signal station, to the large cross at the very tip of the promontory.

This was erected in the late 18th century by a local rector, as a navigational aid. There is an inscription on the base. Parts of the promontory, like so many of the county's most beautiful areas, are owned by the National Trust, and thanks to its care, the Dodman is a nesting site for many species of birds, including songbirds and various migrants.

Continue along the coastal path to the eastern side of pretty Hemmick Beach. Just next to the road, the path swings to the right and continues to run alongside the road until it emerges just short of Penare Farm. Turn right on to the road and follow it as it swings to the left through some buildings and climbs a slight hill. At the top of this the road bends to the left and another joins from the right. There is a gate directly ahead. Go through this and then directly across two fields, down to the buildings of Treveague Farm.

The path back to Gorran Haven is well signposted. Turn right into the farm, which is mostly converted barns, then left behind the farmhouse. Go through the gate on the left and along the top of a very steep meadow before descending and crossing a small stream. This path emerges on a paved lane. Go left to the junction with the main road and turn right, returning to the car park.

# 22. Fowey – The Two Ferries Walk

**Route:**          St Catherine's Castle and Readymoney Cove – Fowey –
                    Ferry To Polruan – Lanteglos Parish Church – Pont Pill –
                    'Q' Memorial – Bodinnick Ferry – Fowey.

**Distance:**       5½ miles on the ground, plus two short ferry journeys.

**Time:**           3 hours

**Terrain:**        Easy to moderate. Mostly coastal walking, with a few
                    short but steep climbs.

**Refreshments:** Fowey and Polruan (the town centre of Polruan is not
                    directly on the route).

**Access:**         Fowey is on the A3082 east of St Austell, and the B3269
                    south of Lostwithiel.

**Maps:**           Ordnance Survey Explorer 107 and Ordnance Survey
                    Landranger 201.

Fowey could be described as the quintessential Cornish town. It has
a rich history of battles and smuggling, piracy and politics. This history, combined with the beauty of the banks of Fowey river, which
tumbles from the rocky peaks of Bodmin to the lush, wooded valleys
and creeks of the south coast, has attracted many writers and artists,
who have in turn spread this pretty port's fame worldwide. Daphne
Du Maurier, Arthur Quiller Couch and Kenneth Graham have all
been inspired by the history and landscape of Fowey – so if leaving it
becomes unexpectedly difficult, do not be surprised, you are not the
first!

The start of the walk is on the western edge of the town. From the A3082,
on entering Fowey, take the turning on the right marked 'St Catherine's
Castle and Readymoney Cove'. The road itself is called Hanson Drive.
Continue along here until the second car park on the right, marked for St
Catherine's Castle. From here, follow the track from the car park down
into Readymoney Cove, which is clearly marked.

This cove, more than any other part of Fowey, stands witness to a turbulent
past, involved through the ages with the defence of the realm. As the track

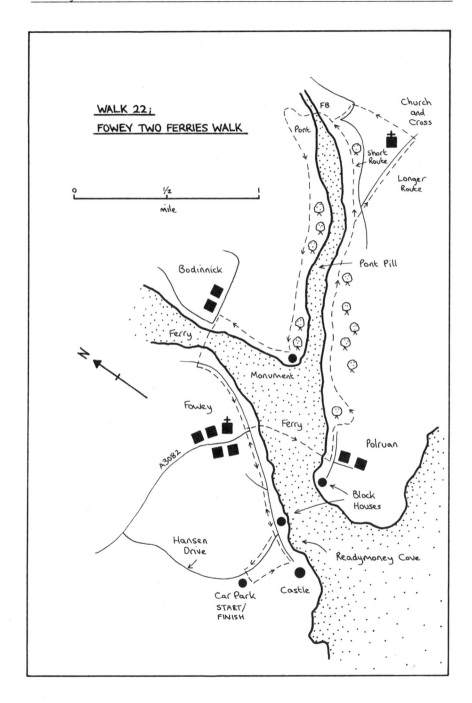

WALK 22;
FOWEY TWO FERRIES WALK

Church and Cross

FB

Pont

Short Route

Longer Route

Pont Pill

Bodinnick

Ferry

Monument

Fowey

Ferry

Polruan

A3082

Block Houses

Hansen Drive

Readymoney Cove

Car Park
START/
FINISH

Castle

0   ½   1
mile

emerges in the cove there is a large house opposite with a plaque on the wall. This is Point Neptune, used by the military during the Second World War.

The castle can be seen on the right of the cove and is owned by English Heritage, with unlimited access for the public. It was built in the 16th century by Henry VIII. St Catherine's was part of a chain of defence which included St Mawes Castle and Pendennis Castle, both of which are in better condition than St Catherine's. This is despite the fact that it was in use until the Second World War, with an 18th-century chart showing the castle had retained a five-gun battery.

**Retrace the route back to Point Neptune and continue along the road into Fowey itself, passing a couple of 'no entry' signs for vehicles. Keep to the seaward road on the right at both this fork and the second one, until passing a chapel on the right and reaching the centre of the town.**

The towers of both St Fim Barr's Church and Place, home of the Treffy family, dominate Fowey. The church is essentially Norman, with an important restoration in 1876. It has been dedicated to three saints in its lifetime, but only that to St Finn Barr has stuck. He was one of many Irish priests who came to Cornwall en route to Brittany and Rome in the mid-Dark Ages. The tower of Place, next to the church, was a 19th-century addition to a 15th-century building and should not be missed. Elizabeth, one of the first Treffys to live there, demonstrated the independent spirit of the town when she managed to defend the house against French raiders in 1457 by pouring molten lead on the heads of her attackers. The house is not open to the public.

**Turn towards the river and walk to the main harbour area by the aquarium. Opposite the large pub called The King of Prussia, a small passenger ferry leaves for Polruan every 15 minutes. A one way trip is approximately 50p.**

As the little boat chugs and rolls across the harbour, the passengers have an excellent view of the remains of the blockhouses on opposite sides of the river. Built in answer to the French raid in 1457, a chain was strung between them to de-mast any unwelcome ships attempting to enter the harbour.

At Polruan, history gives us evidence of how privateering, piracy and politics became enmeshed with the individual nature of Fowey. During the early 19th century, a one-time coastguard of the town called Richard Kingcup left the service and opened an inn. For the next twenty years he smuggled contraband into the county under the noses of the authorities. Many ships used by smugglers were specially built privateers used in the hundred years war, for which Fowey proudly raised the most men in the entire kingdom. After this ended, the boats, which had been constructed with long bowsprits in order to go faster in war, were invaluable to the 'free traders' as they could outstrip any of the revenue cutters in service.

At Polruan harbour, walk up out of the dock area to a phone box at a T-junction. Turn left for a short distance in front of houses, then take the steep stone steps on the right, marked as the footpath to 'the hills'. At the next sign, turn left around the back of a pink house and continue along the path as it leads up out of Polruan and through the woodland on the south bank of Pont Pill. Continue along the path until it is crossed by a track which leads to a private house. Cross this and follow the path down into some woodland, swinging left across a stream. At the next fork in the path, take the route marked to Lanteglos Church.

If preferred this can be missed and a short cut taken straight to Pont Pill, where it joins up with the other route via the church. To do this, stay on the other path until reaching a wooden gate to the road. Go over a stile on the left here, following a path down to Pont, where it meets the longer route.

To reach Lanteglos church, turn right on to the path signposted and continue until it reaches a small gate to a lane. Turn left, then take the first road on the right. From the brow of the hill, the graceful and timeless tower of St Wyllow, the parish church of Lanteglos, is looked down upon.

It stands alone, enfolded in green hills, on a site as old as Christianity itself. The present structure dates from the 13th century and is Grade I listed. There is a lantern cross in the churchyard. Inside, the original 'wagon' roof protects heraldic pew ends which date back 450 years and some rare examples of medieval windows in the north aisle. It was in this small, peaceful church that Daphne Du Maurier married in 1932. She also used it as Lanoc in *The Loving Spirit*.

To continue along the route, walk through the small, white gate in the north-east corner of the churchyard. A small path winds down through some woods to a road. Turn left, then almost immediately on the right is a footpath marked to the footbridge.

The alternative shorter path joins the path here from the left. Cross the bridge over the pill, meaning 'creek' in Cornish.

This picturesque corner is owned by the National Trust and has been sensitively restored.

*Lantern cross, Lanteglos church*

On the opposite side, the path swings right, up the bank, then a fork appears. Turn left, along the path which follows the pill back to the Fowey river. This section roller-coasts towards the mouth of the creek, with some excellent views through the trees.

Nothing compares, however, with the view at Penleath Point, by the memorial to Arthur Quiller-Couch. Fortunately, there are several benches on which to rest and absorb the magnificent bird's-eye view of Fowey and its river, as it winds past Polruan, the blockhouses, the castle and finally out into the ocean.

Arthur Quiller-Couch settled in Fowey, using it, like so many others, in his novels. Visitors many recognise it as Troy Town in his works. He wrote several novels and short stories and edited The Oxford Book Of English Verse. Prominent not only for his writing in Cornwall, he was a professor of English at Cambridge and respected by all who knew him, as is clear from the inscription on his memorial stone. Arthur Quiller-Couch was a great friend of Daphne Du Maurier, who listened to the older writer and his advice on more than one occasion.

Continue along the path which runs parallel to Fowey on the opposite bank. As the path reaches the road at Bodinnick, turn left down to the ferry, which runs regularly until 8:30pm or dusk.

It was in a house called Ferryside, here in Bodinnick, that Daphne Du Maurier lived whilst in her early twenties. Through one long winter of rain and fog she stayed alone in the house, writing her first novel The Loving Spirit, in which she used the history of the place around her to create the atmosphere for which her books are so famous.

The present ferry gives no hint of its ancient history: there has been a ferry here since Norman times.

On the Fowey side, turn left across the car park and follow the road into the centre of town. The easiest route back to the car park is probably to retrace the route, taking the road south past the chapel and climbing back towards the cove on the same road as the start of the walk. However, instead of continuing straight at the last fork by the 'no entry' signs and walking via Readymoney again, stay on the road as it curves up to the right. The car park will be seen a short distance later on the left.

# 23. Duloe

| | |
|---|---|
| **Route:** | Duloe Stone Circle – St Cuby's Church – River Walk – St Nonna's Well – Duloe. |
| **Distance:** | 6 miles |
| **Time:** | 3½ hours |
| **Terrain:** | Moderate to challenging. Mostly woodland and small tracks or lanes, with several steep climbs and descents. The path through the woodland will be very boggy in parts after any rain. |
| **Refreshments:** | Duloe |
| **Access:** | Duloe is on the B3254 between Liskeard and Looe. If using public transport, there is access from both Looe and Liskeard. See end of chapter for details. |
| **Maps:** | Ordnance Survey Explorer 107 St Austell and Liskeard, Ordnance Survey Landranger 201. |

This walk starts and finishes in the small village of Duloe, which lies above a tranquil, wooded valley between the ever popular coastal town of Looe and the wild expanse of Bodmin Moor. The name Duloe has several meanings, all based on the existence of the two rivers which converge and empty into Looe harbour – this walk meanders along part of the West Looe river. For such a small place, Duloe has many features of interest including a mysterious stone circle, which is where this walk starts.

There is a car park in Duloe, a few hundred metres north of the church, opposite the shop. If starting from here, walk down the road towards the church until you reach a large sign on the left indicating the short track which leads up a lane and across a field to the stone circle.

There are hundreds of stone circles in varying conditions all across the country. Duloe, however, is quite possibly unique. It is unusually small – only seven stones remain upright, with one fallen. Yet this is not its most distinctive feature. All eight stones are made of white quartz and, at over two metres, are the tallest such stones in the county. Only a few, apparently

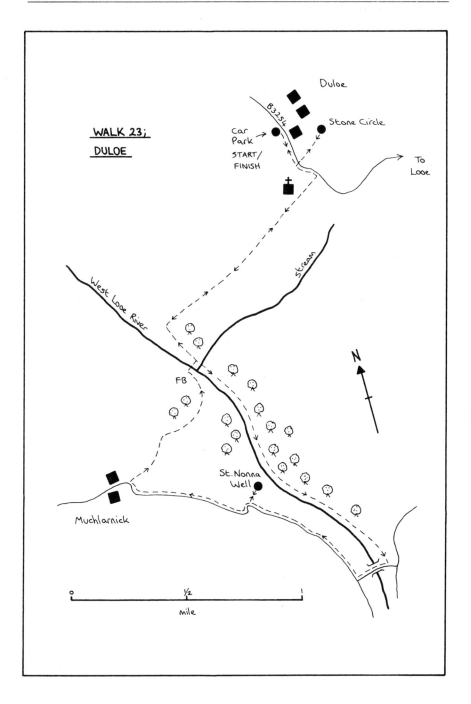

WALK 23;
DULOE

Duloe

B3254

Car Park →

START/
FINISH

Stone Circle

To Looe

West Looe River

Stream

N

FB

Muchlarnick

St. Nonna Well

0    ½    1
mile

carefully selected stones are also quartz, such as one on the south-west corner of Boscawen-un Stone Circle in Penwith (see Land's End Peninsula chapter). It is possible that during the Bronze Age, when this circle was built, quartz was considered to have healing qualities. This does not, however, bring us any closer to an answer as to the circles' original purpose.

In 1860 the circle was restored and a bisecting hedge removed. During this work, a burial urn was found at the base of one of the stones and a solid gold necklace, called the Duloe Torque, which dates from the same period as the circle, was found in a nearby field.

**Retrace the route back to the road and cross over to the church.**

This is dedicated to St Cuby, a native Cornishman who was trained for the priesthood in Ireland during the fifth century, before founding the monastery of Holyhead in Anglesey. An ancient well which also bears his name, but which was probably sacred in the pre-Christian era also, lies a few hundred metres along the Looe road, on the right hand side.

The church itself is of great interest, not least because during the boom in smuggling during the 18th and 19th centuries, Duloe was one of the few inland sites used for the storing of contraband and it was this church which sheltered the booty! So much of it, in fact, that the weight caused subsidence on one side! The present structure dates from the 14th century, although the south tower is slightly earlier. As with many Cornish churches, it is very likely that an early Celtic chapel stood on this site before the building of the Norman church.

However, the oldest and most significant object in the church is the pre-Christian font, which was found under the well when the road was built during the last century. On one side the font bears a carving of a griffin, a symbol in Greek and Roman mythology of evil; the opposite side bears a fish, symbolising purification. As it was obviously used in Christian rites, it would appear that the pagan carvings, like much else of the older religion, were appropriated for the new.

On leaving the church, turn right and walk down the lane marked as unsuitable for vehicles. After a short while this degenerates into a rutted track and descends steeply into the valley. At the bottom, another track joins from the right. The path then comes to a stream. Turn left and cross it, so the water is on the right. There is an avenue of trees with a tempting path running down it on the left. A few metres down this there is a large gap in the hedge on the right and a waymarker post with a yellow arrow

*Celtic font in the church of St Cuby, Duloe*

pointing diagonally across the field. Follow this on to a path which runs on the left bank of the river along the valley floor, with occasional further waymarkers along the route.

This is the West Looe river. The pretty, wooded banks, with impossibly steep fields above, make a perfect setting for a peaceful ramble. Most visitors flock to the Kilminorth Woods just north of Looe, so any walkers are likely to have this tranquil spot to themselves. The woods are particularly lovely in the golden afternoon sun of late autumn.

The woods end as a lane crosses the river at Sowdens Bridge. Climb up to this road, turning right, then right again at the T-junction, climbing the side of the valley. Soon the woodland is far below and the roads makes a hairpin bend to the left. On the corner of this is a track down to Hobb Park Farm, marked as private property. However, a few metres down the track is a sign indicating the short path through a field to St Nonna's Well. Go through the small gate on the right, then walk along the top of the field, next to the hedge. The well is surrounded by a wooden fence.

St Nonna was probably the aunt of St Cuby and this well also dates to the 5th century, although the bowl is probably older. There are many legends connected with this well, including a guardian elf and a curse on removing the bowl, which is always mysteriously full but never overflowing. The gift of a pin to the elf, or piskey, is said to bring good fortune or even divination.

**Retrace the path back up to the road and continue uphill.**

At the next hairpin bend, there is a field on the left which is marked as being a site for a fort, although there is nothing to be seen now.

**Follow the lane into the hamlet of Muchlarnick and take a track on the right as the lane bends to the left. This runs down an increasingly steep side of the valley, eventually emerging at the stream which was crossed earlier. Use the wooden footbridge on the left to cross this time and climb up the original lane, not forgetting to keep to the right as the track forks. The track then returns to the church at Duloe and the start of the walk.**

# 24. Mount Edgcumbe and Kingsand

**Route:** Kingsand – Maker Church – St Julian's Well – Mount Edgcumbe – Kingsand.

**Distance:** 6 miles

**Time:** 3 hours

**Terrain:** Easy. Well-marked and maintained paths on farmland and coast, with one moderate climb.

**Refreshments:** Kingsand, Cremyll.

**Access:** From the A374, take the B3247 for Millbrook and follow the signs for Kingsand. There is limited parking at Kingsand.

**Map:** Ordnance Survey Explorer 108, Ordnance Survey Landranger 201.

This little corner of the county barely qualifies for a guide to Cornwall. It was part of Devon until the middle of the last century, as an original anomaly had become strategically significant over the years. The promontory is certainly worthy of its inclusion, however, as it has some lovely walking, with a great variety of features of interest along the way, many reflecting the area's historic role at the forefront of our naval history.

Kingsand is an attractive little village which grew out of the fishing industry. Yet most of its history is associated with military activity of one sort or another, the entire promontory being home to forts dating from the Iron Age to the present day. However, Kingsand's heyday and the period to which many of the best buildings belong was the 18th and 19th centuries. This was due to an industry which dwarfed fishing and laughed in the face of the huge naval presence: smuggling. Many of the 'free traders' as they called themselves were women, transporting brandy in skins hidden under their skirts, or disguising the brandy as babies. In the early 1800s, it was estimated that almost 17 000 casks of spirits were smuggled through here every year.

*Mount Edgcumbe*

As the road enters Kingsand, turn left at the fork, following the parking signs. There is a small lane on the left just before the car park. The lane is called Earl's Drive and is the start of the walk. This seemingly harmless little lane climbs several hundred feet, passing the now abandoned Grenville Battery. Continue along the road, past Maker Farm on the right. Take the right fork after the farm, then follow the footpath sign on the left across two fields, a concrete track and alongside the garden of the former vicarage, now called Friary Manor. The path then crosses two fields, close to the hedge on the left. Cross a stile and continue along the opposite side of the same hedge.

Almost immediately Maker church comes into sight, as does a wonderful panorama down across the sound to Torpoint and Plymouth. Maker church was almost entirely rebuilt in the 15th century. However, it probably dates from the early Dark Ages as the missionary saints who travelled across the county from Ireland and Wales often built their chapels near wells which were significant for pagan worship, such as St Julian's Well nearby. The earliest mention of it is later, in a letter written by the Bishop of Exeter in 1186, which refers to the church as being part of an Augustinian priory. The unusual

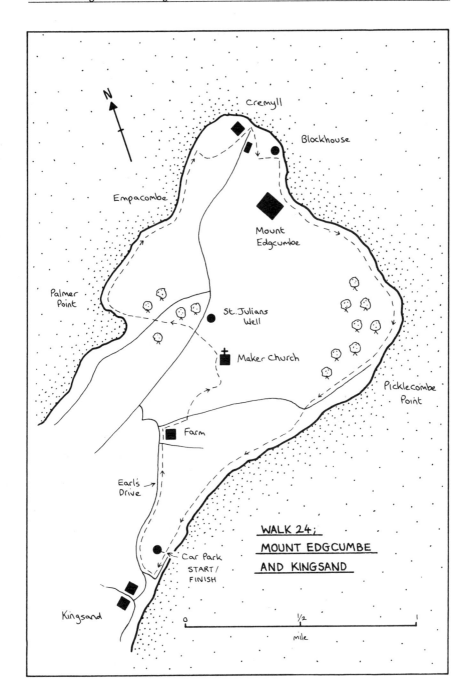

N

Cremyll

Blockhouse

Empacombe

Mount
Edgcumbe

Palmer
Point

St. Julians
Well

Maker Church

Picklecombe
Point

Farm

Earl's
Drive

WALK 24;
MOUNT EDGCUMBE
AND KINGSAND

Car Park
START /
FINISH

Kingsand

0                    ½                    1

mile

name may refer to the Celtic word 'magor' meaning 'ruin', or 'old walls'. It is, however, dedicated to St Julian, who is appropriately the patron saint of ferrymen, considering its proximity to Cremyll ferry.

Like most things in the area, even the church has something of a military history. In the Civil War, the 21-metre tower was fortified during the siege of Plymouth, and in 1644 was raided by the Parliamentarians, who also captured Cawsand fort. In the following century, the tower was again used for military purposes, this time as an Admiralty signalling station. The church now contains a copy of the signal codes used.

The footpath sign to Empacombe is outside the front of the church and points downhill to the main road to Cremyll. Less than 100 metres from the point where the path crosses the road is St Julian's Well (turn right towards Cremyll).

The well is located on a bank by the road and is in good repair as it was restored by the Earl of Edgcumbe in 1882. St Julian was the likely companion of St Samson, who came to Cornwall from Wales some time in the 6th century.

Return to the original crossing and follow the footpath sign on the opposite side of the road into the woods. Continue on the path, zigzagging downhill (do not be tempted to walk along the track which crosses the path). The path emerges from the woods on a grassy slope. Go straight across this, down to the gate which opens on to the lane. Cross this and follow the path around to Palmer Point, which has some pleasant views out across the water.

The path passes a disused windmill which was built to replace the one at Maker Heights, and was one of the last to work in Cornwall.

The paths comes to tiny Empacombe, with the high walls of Mount Edgecumbe gardens sheltering the handful of cottages. Follow the signs around the harbour and go through the gate, continuing along the path which emerges at Cremyll and the entrance to Mount Edgecumbe house and gardens.

This imposing Tudor mansion has been the seat of the Earls of Edgcumbe since the land was granted to the family, which at the time owned Cothele House, by Henry VIII. The house was almost destroyed by German bombs in 1941, but was fully restored ten years later. The 320-hectare (800-acre) estate is very famous for its gardens, which have many different designs and plants from around the world. They have been open to the public for 200 years, and the present Earl of Edgcumbe continues the tradition by opening the house to the public on certain days throughout the summer. The park is open all year and there is no admission charge as it was purchased jointly by Cornwall County Council and Plymouth City Council in 1970.

Enter the park through the main gates, then take the first path on the left, through the formal garden with the fountain. Continue along a wide, concrete track, passing the blockhouse on the right.

The blockhouse was built in the 1500s and matches the fort on the other side of The Narrows. They were built to prevent invaders from gaining further entrance into the Sound by heavily defending the narrowest point in the harbour.

Stay on the path closest to the water, passing a pond and walking up to the Temple Of Milton, a folly built in the 19th century with an inscription from Paradise Lost inside. Follow the path to the left of this, into the woods.

Soon after this you should see a ruin on the skyline. This is not the ancient, romantic ruin it appears to be, but another Victorian folly.

At the next fork in the path, go right, passing a pretty, little cottage that bears a striking resemblance to the Gingerbread House of fairy tales. After this the path rejoins the lower route, then zigzags uphill and through a ruined archway.

This wide, level and pleasant path swings past Picklecombe Point, with its fort built in 1848 and now converted into flats. On the right is a curious and rather dank Gothic chapel seat which looks out through the tangle of woodland, across the fort and out to sea.

Continue along the path until a wooden gate exits on to a road. Go through the wooden gate which is almost opposite, following the route along the now exposed path back into Kingsand. Once in the village, turn right, passing a pub on the left which is housed in a very elegant, three-storey, Georgian townhouse. The car park is a little further along the road on the right.

# Useful Information

**Transport in the South Coast Area:** There are several main line stations in the area. These include Truro, Liskeard, Plymouth and St Austell. Call 0345 484950 for all rail enquires. For local bus timetable information on Western National services in the south-east of the county, call 01752 222666. The Truro area is covered by Truronian, including all buses to Trelissick Gardens (Walk 19). The number for enquires is 01872 273453.

The Plymouth to Cawsand ferry (pedestrian) runs from May to September. The crossing time is 30 minutes. Call 01752 822797 for details. The Bodinnick to Fowey ferry runs all year. Call 01726 870232 for details. The Mount Edgcumbe to Plymouth ferry operates in the summer only. Call 01752 822105. The Polruan-Fowey ferry is open all year. Call 01726 832626.

**Other Information:** Trelissick Gardens, open March to Christmas, 01872 862090. Mount Edgecumbe House is open April to October, Wednesday to Sunday, including bank holidays; the park is open all year, 01752 822236.

**Tourist Information Centres:** Fowey, Post Office, Custom House Hill, 01726 833616. Looe (seasonal), The Guildhall, Fore St., E Looe 01503 262072. Plymouth, Civic Centre, Armada Way, 01752 264849. St Austell, By-Pass, Southbourne Rd., 01726 76333. Truro, Municipal Bldgs., Boscawen St., 01872 74555.

**Youth hostels:** Penquite House, Golant, Fowey, 01726 833507.

# Bodmin
# Moor

*The Cheesewring, Minions: see walk 25*

# 25. Minions

**Route:**         Minions – Hurlers Stone Circles – Daniel Gumb's Cave – Cheesewring Quarry – Stowe's Pound Iron Age Hill Fort (remains) – South Pheonix Mine – Minions.

**Distance:**    2 miles

**Time:**        1 hour

**Terrain:**     Easy. All moorland walking with one short climb to the Cheesewring.

**Access:**      Minions is located on a minor road west of the B3254 at Upton Cross, north of Liskeard. For public transport details, see end of chapter.

**Refreshments:** Minions

**Maps:**        Ordnance Survey Explorer 109 and Ordnance Survey Landranger 201.

This is a short but popular walk on Minions Moor. The easy access to the stone circles in particular mean that this tiny hamlet has two car parks and can be fairly busy during the summer months. However, both the astonishing number and variety of sites of interest in these two short miles demands that this walk be included in the guide. This tiny part of the moor will introduce visitors to a different landscape, one shaped not by roads and cities, but by timeless places of ritual and the necessities of life: survival and death.

At almost 1000ft (304 metres), Minions is the highest village in Cornwall and is thought to have been named after a Celtic king who ruled sometime in the late Dark Ages.

The walk starts in the western car park of the village in Minions. Take the track on the left up to the moor, until an information point can be seen on the right, facing the Hurlers.

These three stone circles have been dated by English Heritage, who own the site, as belonging to the Bronze Age, probably around 1500BC. Their unusual name comes from the legend which states that they are, in fact, men, turned to stone for playing the ancient Cornish game of hurling on a Sunday. This story is strikingly similar to one associated with a stone circle in West

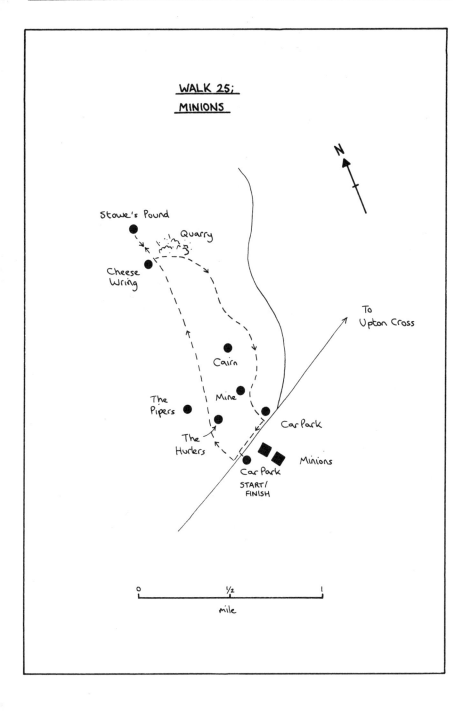

WALK 25;
MINIONS

N

Stowe's Pound

Quarry

Cheese Wring

To
Upton Cross

Cairn

Mine

The Pipers

The Hurlers

Car Park

Minions

Car Park
START/
FINISH

0   ½   1
mile

Cornwall, where girls were turned to stone for dancing on a Sunday. In both cases, the story is probably a Puritan version of a much older myth. Oddly, both circles have two outlying standing stones. The ones by the Hurlers stand together just to the west of the circles, on the right of the track.

Walk through the circles, heading for the rocky hill in the near distance. There are several paths across the moor in the same direction at this point, and it is not important which is taken.

There are many large rocks and slabs of stone scattered about the moor. A quick eye may see that some of these bear evidence of being worked. Before the 19th century, stone was cut by inserting a wedge into a groove cut in the rock. This was far from exact and many abandoned attempts can be seen.

As the path comes closer to the hill, a small cave can be seen centre-left, facing the moor.

This once marked the home of a local philosopher and stone cutter by the name of Daniel Gumb who moved his family to a natural cave in the early 18th century. The cave seen today is a reconstruction of the much larger cave, which was moved about 90 metres to the south-west when quarrying began in the 19th century. On the right of the entrance, Daniel carved his name and the date, 1735. The roof bears geometrical carvings of one of Euclid's problems.

The path up to the Cheesewring is to the left of the cave, with the wire fence bordering the quarry on the right.

The silvery granite of this moor has been sought after for several centuries and quarrying reached its peak in the mid-1800s, when stone from here was used to build many famous landmarks in London, including the Albert Memorial and Tower Bridge. The quarry, however, has its own famous landmark; the Cheesewring. This unusual rock formation stands approximately six metres in height and has been the object of many an excursion in the past two centuries. The unusual name derives from its close resemblance to a cider press, with round, flat stones to squeeze the juice from apple pulp, known locally as 'cheese'. The west side of the quarry is probably the best place to find some stones with wedge and groove markings.

Much of the summit is surrounded by a line of piled rocks. These are not the remains of quarrying, but, more surprisingly, survivors of it. Cheesewring Quarry is part of an Iron Age hill fort called Stowe's Pound. It is quite amazing that anything of this should remain, yet the low perimeter wall extends around the lower summit to the north, enclosing the remains of hut circles. There is an entrance on the western side of the hill, and the northern edge is

The Hurlers

a good viewpoint across the marsh to the remains of an ancient field system on the lower slopes of Sharptor. Stowe's Pound is one of several such hill forts built around the edges of the moor. Berry Down, which is visited in the St Neot walk, uses the natural rock formations and contours of the hill as an integral part of the defences, and the people who built Stowe's Pound used the same ingenious method.

Don't, however, become so involved in Stowe's Pound that the descent is made before taking in the magnificent views! To the east lies Dartmoor, a brown line on the horizon over twenty miles away. Over twice the distance further and to the north, Exmoor can just been seen on a clear day. A distant shimmer on the horizon belies the south Cornish coast, and far to the west stand the massive white antennae of Goonhilly Earth Satellite Station on the Lizard Peninsula.

Also to be seen from the summit when facing south is a mound atop a low hill in the middle distance, between Stowe's Pound and Minions. This mound shelters Rillaton Barrow, a Bronze Age burial chamber which was excavated in 1837 and yielded a priceless gold cup dating from the same time as the Hurlers. Also found were a skeleton, a dagger and some pottery. A copy of the cup can be found in the Truro County Museum.

**Leave the summit by descending on the path next to the fence on the south side of the quarry, heading for the track on the left which lies between the two fenced off areas at the base of the Pound.**

The granite sleepers of the Liskeard Caradon Railway can be seen here. It was extended in 1877 to run from Stowe's Pound down to Looe, from where the granite was shipped. Further remains could be seen until 1984, when much was destroyed in the search for suitable rock to repair a Plymouth breakwater.

**This track joins a wider track on the left and continues down towards Minions. As it reaches a house surrounded by trees, there is a mine building on the right.**

This is South Phoenix Mine, restored in 1991, 110 years after being built. The Caradon Mines were the centre of the copper boom in the 19th century and also produced large quantities of tin, employing hundreds of men, women and children. The restored mine building now houses a free exhibition on the history of mining in the area.

**After leaving the exhibition, follow the path on the south side of the building past the house and into the car park. Turn right along the road, through the village, to return to the western car park and the start of the walk.**

# 26. St Neot

**Route:** St Neot Church – Trengale Woods – Berry Down Fort (remains) – Holy Well – St Neot.

· **Distance:** 4¾ miles

**Time:** 2½ hours

**Terrain:** Moderate. The walk includes woodland, farmland and moorland and is very steep in places, although the path is always well defined.

**Refreshments:** St Neot

**Access:** St Neot is accessed by a B road signposted off the A 38 west of Dobwalls. Access from other directions is by minor roads only.

**Maps:** Ordnance Survey Explorer 109 Bodmin Moor.

This walk includes a section of the Two Valleys Walk, which has largely been waymarked with posts showing an arrow and a green circle (although not always in the most useful of places!). It includes much of interest in the Bodmin area, including the variety of land-scape, without requiring a lonely hike across miles of moorland. Starting in the pretty church town of St Neot, the route crosses green pastures and wooded valleys before climbing up to the magnificent viewpoint of Berry Down Fort.

From the car park in the centre of the village, turn right across the River Loveny, using the 18th-century bridge.

This suffered somewhat when the road was widened, but is charming none-theless.

A few minutes walk and St Neot's Church is on the left.

This church has several objects of interest, any one of which would justify a visit in its own right. The church itself was built in the 15th century and is one of the best examples of its period in the area. However, the list of vicars dates to 1266, and the arrival of the Normans two centuries earlier had led to the closing of a priory which stood on the site at the time. The church gets it name from St Neot, widely believed to have been a Saxon and relative of King Alfred. It is more probable, however, that Neot was one of many Dark Age saints who spread Christianity throughout the country in the face of the barbarian Saxon invasion from the east. At this time the village was known as St Anietus. The holy man who healed Alfred after a hunting trip in the area was called Gueryr. In the written account of this, Neot's name was added after, by a different hand.

The most striking of the many interesting points inside the church are the 16th-century stained glass windows, which are priceless. The earliest and least restored is the Creation Window at the east end of the south aisle. Many of the other windows show local benefactors with their favourite saints. Also of great interest are the five ancient crosses located outside the main entrance. The tallest of these is a fine example dating from the 10th century with intricate Celtic carvings on all four sides of the shaft (sadly, the head is missing). Three of the others are 15th century, and the fourth is a lantern cross from St Kew.

*Celtic crosses, St Neot's churchyard*

From the church, the route continues up the road out of the village, ignoring the turn on the right on the main road. This is a fairly steep climb, but levels out at the junction with the remains of a Celtic cross on the left. This

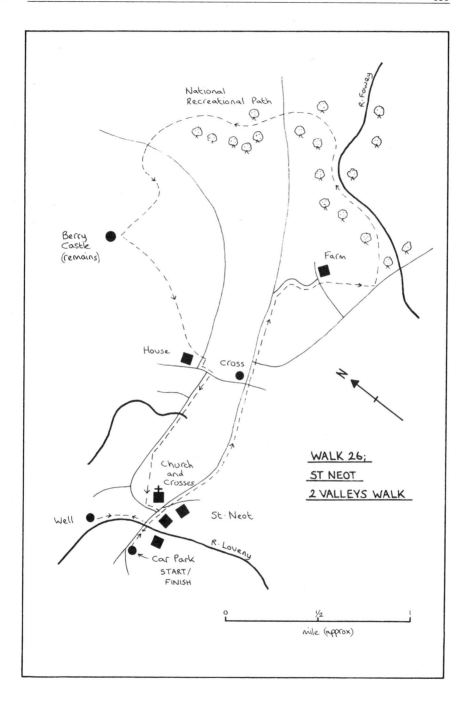

is where the path joins up with the waymarked route. Again, continue straight, until a few metres later, where there is a fork. Go left down this tiny country lane, taking the next right down a track. This emerges on another lane, opposite a farm. Follow the footpath sign over the stile (not down the driveway), cutting diagonally left down a very steep field. At the bottom, go left along the fence and into the trees to the wooden stile on the right, then immediately over another stile on the left, following a path through the woodland by the side of the River Fowey.

> These are the pretty Trengale Woods, which further upstream contain the rapids of the beautiful Golitha Falls.

The path continues by the side of the river, which swings in a wide arc to the right. Eventually, the path reaches a set of steps with a metal handrail. Go down these and follow the wide path until it turns to the left, away from the river, and crosses a field. The exit is on the left, through the gate. Go up to the road and cross it, following the footpath sign on the left across another field and into more woodland.

> This part of the walk is simply perfect on a late autumn afternoon, with the sun slanting through the dying leaves, brilliant with colour.

This path climbs steadily up until it enters an open field, which it goes straight across, using the gates. In the third field, just before the buildings, exit over the stile on the right into woods. After a few metres, these open on to a road. Turn right, then left at the fork, following the road as it climbs up the side of Berry Down. Follow the sign on the left onto the hill and take the path on the left, climbing the nearside of the summit. This path skirts the side of the hill, but there are several smaller paths which climb up to the top.

> The extra effort is rewarded with magnificent views in all directions. It is not difficult to see why this site was chosen as a defensive position. Similar hill forts were built all around the edges of the moor. Berry Down, like Stowe's Pound near Minions, uses natural formations of rock in its defences, although parts of the ditch and rampart system of defences can clearly be seen as they stand up to 1.5 metres high. There are also eight hut circles inside the protective walls. The whole enclosure lies on the southern aspect of the summit, protected from the north wind. At first glance, the enclosure may appear to be typically Iron Age, but it's possible that the enclosure dates from the Bronze, or even Neolithic era.

The main entrance is on the south side, sweeping down the hill towards

St Neot. Go through this, down to the wall. There is a stile over this, slightly to the left and partly hidden by some trees.

This part of the path is on the so-called Dragon Path, a system of trade routes dating from the Neolithic period, linking Glastonbury Tor with Land's End. The unusual name is due to the fact that the route passes by several churches dedicated to St Michael the Archangel, who fought a dragon.

The path continues along this route, crossing the field to the far right corner, then goes over a stile into another, longer field. Cross this and exit over the stile just to the left of the house. Once on the lane, turn right, then at the junction go left, taking the next road on the right and re-joining the waymarked route. Continue along this until it forks by the buildings. Take the road on the left and continue down to the farm. Here there is another fork, with a track on the left. This is a short cut into the village. The track ends on a lane, where you go left into the village centre. Do not hurry back to the car park, however! Turn right along the village street, then right again by the garage, following the signs for the holy well. This track goes up to a level meadow by the River Loveny. Over on the right, the large Victorian well house can be seen.

This houses St Neot's well. Early Christian saints often located their churches near wells which became 'holy', but whose healing powers were invariably pre-Christian. As late as 1833 it is recorded that sick children were taken there to benefit from the well's healing properties. At many other holy wells, the pagan custom of tying rags and other offerings on nearby hawthorn trees to invoke the well's curative powers is practised to this day.

From here, re-trace the path back to the village centre and continue on over the bridge, back to the car park.

---

# 27. Cardinham

---

**Route:**        Cardinham Church and Crosses – Cardinham Moor –
               Bury Castle (remains) – Inscribed Stones – Cardinham
               Castle (remains) – Cardinham.

**Distance:**     4¾ miles

**Time:**         2¼ hours

**Terrain:**      Easy to moderate, with one long but undemanding climb.

**Refreshments:** None are available on the route.

**Access:**       The village is located on a minor road east of the A30, just
               north of Bodmin town.

**Maps:**         Ordnance Survey Explorer 109 and Ordnance Survey
               Landranger 200.

---

This is a pleasant walk which climbs from the old Celtic church town of Cardinham, with its fine church and crosses, up to the edge of the moor, a climb which is rewarded by fine views north across the moor and south down the wooded valleys to the sea. There are several sites of interest along the route and the path passes through varied terrain, including some ancient ways.

The walk starts in Cardinham which, like many similar parishes in this part of the county, has a tiny hamlet at its centre, with larger communities elsewhere in the parish. The church itself is worth a visit, not least for the two very impressive crosses in the churchyard, one of which was rescued from being used as part of the church wall!

The church claims that the cross with Scandinavian markings outside the porch door is the finest in England, and there is no doubt that it makes a strong challenge for the title. The other cross is equally interesting, however, as it is mounted on an inscribed stone dating from the Romano-British era, whilst the cross itself dates from AD900, one hundred years younger than the other cross. The church is 15th century and seems to have survived the Victorian craze for meddling with such things relatively intact. It is dedicated to St Meubred, a 5th-century Irish saint who came to a rather sticky end, managing to get himself beheaded in Rome.

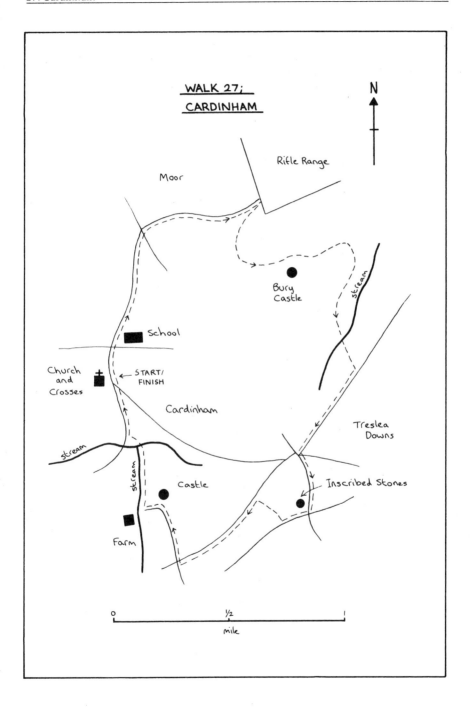

From the church, walk in a northerly direction down the road and continue straight at the junction, passing the school on the right. This is the start of the long climb up to Bury Castle. At the next T-junction, go left, then take the first right. The road is mainly used for access to the army firing range, but is otherwise fairly neglected, and it is not long before the road is just an unfenced strip across the moor. There are sheep and ponies wandering freely, so keep dogs under control.

At the end of the road there is a gate and fence bordering the military area. Ignore the footpath sign pointing around the edge of the enclosure and turn about 180 degrees to the right. There is a path about one metre wide which cuts through the gorse on the (now) left of the road. Take this route and keep the stone hedge on the left as the moor narrows to the size of a field. After a few minutes, another wall forms a right angle with the one on the left and there is a gate in the corner. Go through this (a marker is helpfully placed out of sight on the other side). Cross the small enclosure, using a stile in the far left corner. The next field has a waymarker at the top left corner by the gate, but there's no stile.

> The remains of Bury Castle now come into plain view on the right. This north-western corner has the most impressive remains of the ditch and rampart defences, standing up to several metres at the highest point. This is an Iron Age fort, one of several to ring the edge of the moor. The outline of the entire fort can clearly be seen, its size suggesting that it was one of the more important forts, almost certainly more important than the nearby Berry Down Fort at St Neot. However, unlike several others, it was probably not re-occupied during the Dark Ages.

The walk continues over a stile in the north-east corner of the fort. To find this, walk straight along the edge of the outer rampart from the previous waymarker and the stile can be seen a few metres further on, just as the hill starts to slope downwards. Cross this and continue down the old, walled green lane which runs down the side of the field. This emerges on a track. Turn right and follow it through the wood. Cross the cattle grid and stay on the track until it reaches a lane which runs along the tops of Treslea Downs. Turn right on to this road and head back towards Cardinham. At the next junction, take the second road on the left, which has a footpath sign by the side of the road after a few metres (ignore it and stay on the road). Continue walking down the lane until the crossroads.

> On the right, set high up in the hedge, are two inscribed stones dating from the sixth or seventh century. Both have been moved from their original positions, one having previously stood against the wall of a farm building at Well-

*Celtic cross and Cardinham Church*

town. They both have Latin inscriptions which are almost impossible to decipher, although one almost certainly says 'Vilathus, son of Urochanus', a memorial, in all likelihood, to someone of prominence in the area at the time, although there are no official records of those mentioned.

Turn right at these crossroads and continue until a footpath sign on the right.

Cross two fields, keeping the hedge on the right, and go through a rusty, old gate on to a road. Turn left and continue until a junction appears and a road on the right is marked as the bridleway to Cardinham. Take this road, following it around as it swings to the left.

On the right at this point is the bare outline of what remains of a Norman motte and bailey castle built by the fitz-Turolds, first of the Lords of Cardinham. It lay in ruins three hundred years later, never having been attacked. Legend links Cardinham to the Caadigan of Arthurian times and there was, indeed, an older, pre-Norman castle whose earthworks are just to the south of the motte and bailey. If this were a castle which was occupied at the time of Arthur in the early Dark Ages, it might explain why Bury Castle was not re-inhabited at that time.

After the road has swung to the left, a few metres further on, there is a house on the right. On the far side of this a small track on the right runs down the side of the house, leading through a farm gate (do not go through the smaller gate, marked Beware of the Dog!) Continue straight between the farm buildings, keeping the stream on the left. Once into the meadow, keep to the path as it climbs up to the hedge on the right, then descends through the wood and crosses a stream. Continue along the walled path which swings to the left, then goes through a gate. This leads into the yard of a house, then on to the road. Turn right and the church can be seen a few minutes further up the road.

# 28. The Four Tors Walk

**Route:** Candra – King Arthur's Hall – Stone Circle – Garrow Tor – Brown Willy – Stone Circles – Middle Moor Cross – Candra.

**Distance:** 8¼ miles

**Time:** 5 hours

**Terrain:** Moderate to challenging. Moorland walking with some climbs.

**Refreshments:** None available on the route.

**Access:** The route starts at the end of the public road at Candra, 1½ miles east of St Breward.

**Map:** Ordnance Survey Explorer 109 Bodmin Moor. A map is strongly recommended for this walk, as is a compass.

This walk may be one of the most challenging in the book, but it is also one of the most rewarding. The route crosses one of Britain's last wildernesses, climbing to the county's highest point. Bodmin is a wild, lonely and often haunting landscape, where the remains of civilisations whose people walked this land lie close to the surface. During the Bronze Age, the climate here was more temperate and the moor was densely populated. These people have left their homes and places of ritual for us to see and puzzle over, and several such sites lie along this route.

From the end of the road at Candra, follow the wall on the right up to the moor. After a very short distance, this becomes a waymarked path going east across Emblance Downs, towards the fenced off King Arthur's Hall.

This peculiar enclosure probably dates from the late Neolithic or early Bronze Age and has confounded historians and archaeologists as to its use. The enclosure is 48 by 20 metres, with an entrance in the north-east corner facing Garrow Tor, an area populated for many centuries. The name of the building which once stood here links it, of course, to the most famous and persistent legend in the entire nation – that of King Arthur.

The huge number of monuments and places bearing his name rules out the notion that this was literally his hall, yet in a time of many wars, such as the Dark Ages, the use of a leader's name in connection with a settlement would signal allegiance, thereby drawing the lines of conflict. This might go some way to explaining the number of castles and settlements the great warrior is supposed to have lived in throughout the West Country and Wales!

Continue on the path east towards the woodland at the base of Garrow Tor, following the field wall on the left. At this point, a poorly preserved stone circle, the first of many, can be seen on the right. The path crosses a stile and goes through the trees, emerging on the tor and swinging right, around the base.

This tor bears the remains of many settlements on its slopes. The earliest date from the Bronze Age, and the hut circles can easily be seen on the left of the path as it cuts across the south side of the hill. Several of the walls stand to a height which makes it easy to visualise the community layout here, and which existed for almost two thousand years. Excavations have produced many household items, such as pottery and beads. The tor also bears witness to the medieval period, when 'platform houses' were built, with a room dug into the side of the hill and a platform for the animals constructed at the opposite end.

As the path approaches an abandoned farmhouse, turn right down to the bottom of the valley and cross the De Lank river.

This name comes not, as one might assume, from Norman influence, but from the Celtic word 'dhu' meaning 'black', and reflects the nature of the this moody and often unsettling landscape.

Continue to follow the marker posts up Butter's Tor, swinging to the left about halfway up and once again skirting the summit. This path then descends the opposite slope and crosses a stream via a footbridge. Cross the track and climb straight up the side of Brown Willy ridge on the other side, following the markers. Fortunately, this is the lower end of the ridge. The path then takes a 90-degree turn to the left, following the line of the ridge up to the absolute summit of Cornwall, with the trig point marking the spot.

Brown Willy, from the Cornish for 'high' or 'conspicuous' hill (obviously our forefathers had a taste for understatement), stands 1365ft (420 metres) above sea level, towering above even the high moorland, and can be seen from Dartmoor on a clear day. Two massive cairns mark the top of the hill. One actually forms the base of the triangulation pillar, standing around

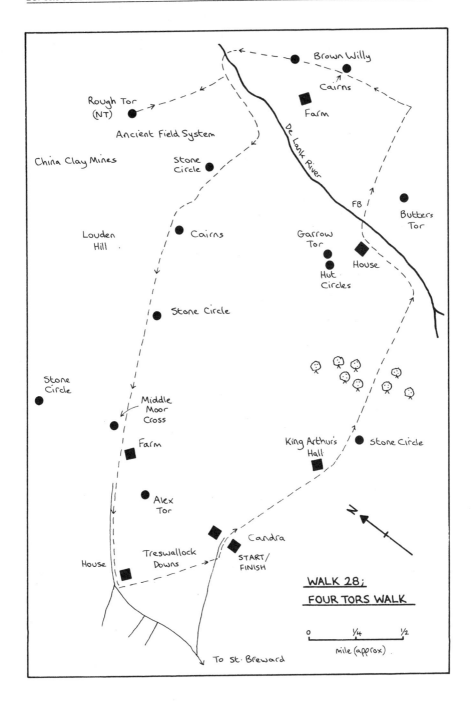

Brown Willy

Cairns

Rough Tor
(NT)

Farm

Ancient Field System

De Lank River

China Clay Mines

Stone
Circle

FB

Butters
Tor

Louden
Hill

Cairns

Garrow
Tor

House

Hut
Circles

Stone Circle

Stone
Circle

Middle
Moor
Cross

King Arthur's
Hall

Stone Circle

Farm

Alex
Tor

Candra

House

Treswallock
Downs

START/
FINISH

**WALK 28;
FOUR TORS WALK**

N

To St. Breward

0        ¼        ½

mile (approx).

3 metres high and 25 metres across. The other is on the southern end of the top ridge and stands to just under 2 metres in height.

To the north is Rough Tor, perhaps one of the most famous on Bodmin, and protected by the National Trust, with open access for the general public. The summit is crowned by a memorial to the men of the 43rd Wessex Division, and, at the northern base, a monument to the murdered girl, Charlotte Diamond. Everything else on the tor is pre-historic and includes enclosures, ancient field systems and cairns.

From the magnificent viewpoint of Brown Willy, descend the north slope on a path which crosses a stile, then swings left and again crosses the De Lank river, going through a gate with a notice stating that the path to Brown Willy is a permissive path only. Straight ahead is Rough Tor, offering the possibility of a diversion, if so wished. The entire tor is open to the public, as it is in the ownership of the National Trust. The walk, however, continues along a poorly-defined path, but you should simply stick to the wall on the left and follow it past some woodland and down to a track. On the left is a private farm and entry is forbidden.

This is Fernacre, a farm whose earliest record dates back to 1327. It is also one of the most remote places still inhabited on the moor. Many such isolated farms were worked until about fifty years ago, but have since been abandoned and left to fall into ruin, such as the house passed on the east slope of Garrow Tor earlier in the walk.

As the path reaches the track, turn right and follow it across King Arthur's Downs in the direction of St Breward.

Several stone circles lie along this part of the route, the first of which is Fernace Circle which appears almost immediately on the right. It dates from the early part of the Bronze Age era, making it one of the oldest circles in the country. Many of the stones remain upright to a height of about one metre and the maximum diameter is over 40 metres. The shape is not, however, strictly circular. One side is noticeably flattened, something it has in common with the Stannon circle, also located on the right of the track, but set further back, towards the china clay mines. Both circles contain more stones than other circles on the moor and their layout seems less methodical. The latter circle cannot be seen from here, nor can any of the other circles in this part of the moor.

It is unclear as to what these monuments were used for and speculation on this subject has generated theories which range from the mundane to the frankly bizarre. Generally, however, it is agreed that the circles had some sort of ritualistic or civic purpose.

As the track approaches Louden Hill on the right, there are two cairns on the left of the track.

These are Bronze Age burial chambers. Stone cists of various sizes would contain the remains of a person, probably a chief or leader, often with some objects from his earthly domain, such as pottery or beads (quite common finds in excavated cairns). The stone structure would then be covered with a mound of earth. The construction, of course, varies from area to area and develops throughout the period.

As the track gets closer to the village and fields begin to take over from open moorland, a large cross comes into view, just before a farm on the left.

*The author at the summit of Brown Willy. Roughtor is in the background.*

This is Middle Moor Cross, the most remote cross on Bodmin. It also one of the most interesting. It is a wheel-headed wayside cross, placed here to act as a guide along this route (which has ancient origins) across the moor. The fact the cross has nothing more than a rough, incised mark on each face suggests an early date, probably somewhere around the mid-Dark Ages. There is a legend in the locality that the cross spins until it falls when it hears the church bells from St Breward, and it was, indeed, found on its side in the mid-1900s and again in the early part of this century.

Continue along the track, which becomes a tarmac lane just past the farm (cars are not allowed past this point on the moor). As this reaches a junction, there is a footpath sign on the left. Take this across three fields, past the house (not up the driveway) and through a gate in the final field on to Treswallock Downs. Climb the hill and down below on the right is Candra. From the brow of the hill, swing right to join the road and continue down into the hamlet.

# Useful Information

**Transport in the Bodmin Area:** This is the most difficult section in the guide to explore using public transport. The area's remote beauty is reflected in and possibly maintained by its lack of accessibility. There are no bus services to Minions (Walk 25), Cardinham (Walk 27) or St Breward (Walk 28). There is one bus per day to St Neot from Bodmin, call 01208 79898 for details. The nearest train station is Bodmin Parkway, call 0345 484950 for all rail enquires.

**Other Information:** The majority of paths recommended in this section of the guide follow waymarked routes which are public rights of way. Bodmin Moor is a common to which only the residents have rights and should be regarded as private property. However, walkers who follow the Country Code are generally tolerated, provided they do not enter any parts of the moor which have been enclosed. Bodmin is the wildest and most remote part of the county, and walking here can be a wonderful experience. It can also be dangerous, so it is vital that the correct clothing, adequate food and water, a map and a compass are taken when walking in the area.

**Tourist Information Centres:** Bodmin, Shire House, Mount Folly, 01208 76616.

# More Cornish books from Sigma Leisure

## BEST PUB WALKS IN CORNWALL

Both coastal and countryside walks are to be found in this excellent book, with a Real Ale pub in every village to be visited.

*£6.95*

## MYTHS & LEGENDS OF CORNWALL

Craig Weatherhill & Paul Devereux

The ancient land of Cornwall is steeped in folklore and mystery - all retold by two leading experts - "Superb guide" THE CAULDRON.

*£6.95*

## CORNISH PLACE NAMES & LANGUAGE

"Probably the most important handbook devoted to the use of the Cornish language in Cornwall's place names" CORNISH WORLD.

*£6.95*

## CYCLING IN DEVON & CORNWALL

These 32 routes promise a different perspective on cycling in Devon and Cornwall as well as gentle, healthy exercise in generally traffic-free conditions."...see over the hedge and enjoy the landscape and wildife whilst making real headway and covering real distances in a reasonable span of time"

*£6.95*